Study Guide and Workbook

to accompany

Cultural Anthropology, eighth edition

William A. Haviland

Prepared by Cynthia Keppley Mahmood
University of Maine

Harcourt Brace College Publishers

Fort Worth Philadelphia San Diego New York Orlando Austin San Antonio
Toronto Montreal London Sydney Tokyo

Address for editorial correspondence:
Harcourt Brace College Publishers, 301 Commerce Street, Suite 3700, Ft. Worth, Texas 76102.

Address for orders:
Harcourt Brace & Company 6277 Sea Harbor Drive, Orlando, Florida 32887-6777, 1-800-782-4479 or 1-800-435-0001 (in Florida).

Printed in the United States of America

ISBN: 0-15-502240-7

6 7 8 9 0 1 2 3 4 5 095 9 8 7 6 5 4 3 2 1

Table of Contents

Introduction:
Why Should You Use the Study Guide and Workbook?

Your instructor may or may not require the use of this Study Guide and Workbook to accompany William Haviland's text, *Cultural Anthropology*, Eighth Edition. However, there are some important reasons why you might find it helpful as you begin your study of cultural anthropology.

First of all, using a study guide and workbook along with the main text for the course forces you to simply spend time with the material. You have probably found that when you think you have read an assignment for a course, often you actually can't recall much of what you read. By adding time to your reading for answering review questions, going over key vocabulary, and so on, you fix the information in your memory in a far more thorough manner. The time you spend each day on your study guide and workbook will help you to spend less time "cramming" for exams later on.

Second, putting things in your own words, as our Study Guide and Workbook requires, is the best way to make the subject your own. Education researchers agree that this is a good way to ensure that simple memorization is replaced by true comprehension of information. In addition, the exercises which encourage you to grasp concepts rather than memorize words will help you on tests, in which instructors may phrase things in different ways than your textbook author does. Make the book your own; write in it; do the exercises you find useful and skip the ones you don't. I prepared this guide to help *you*.

Each chapter of the Study Guide and Workbook contains several sections. A *synopsis* of the chapter is followed by an outline of *what you should learn from the chapter*. Then comes a section of *key terms and names* for you to define or identify and a list of *review questions* which can be answered in a few sentences. *Fill-in-the-blank* sections will serve as further review of the material. (You can later use these pages to study for tests.) Many chapters also contain *exercises* involving constructing charts or locating cultures on maps.

To help you specifically prepare for exams, there are *multiple-choice practice questions*, *true/false practice questions*, *practice matching sets*, and *practice essays*. All of these are excellent ways of preparing for the various kinds of tests your instructor may prepare.

I hope that you find this book to be a useful complement to the textbook you will be reading. It has been revised after extensive experience with cultural anthropology students at the University of Maine, and with particular help from my student assistant, Anne James. Scott Allen, an earlier student assistant, was also of great help in previous versions of the study guide which we drew on freely.

Cynthia Keppley Mahmood

Chapter 1
The Nature of Anthropology

Synopsis

This chapter introduces the discipline of anthropology, the study of humankind everywhere, throughout time. Anthropology seeks to produce useful generalizations about people and their behavior, to arrive at the fullest possible understanding of human diversity, and to understand those things that all human beings have in common. There are two major subfields of anthropology: physical anthropology and cultural anthropology. Physical anthropology focuses on the biological aspects of being human while cultural anthropology focuses on human beings as members of society. Because of anthropology's holistic perspective, it can contribute substantially to the resolution of human problems.

What You Should Learn from This Chapter

1. Learn how anthropology helps us to better understand ourselves:
   • explore the impulse to find out who we are and where we came from
   • explain how and why the discipline emerged and developed
   • describe anthropology's relationship to the other social sciences
2. Know the subfields of anthropology and understand their purpose and practice:
   • physical anthropology
   • archaeology
   • linguistics
   • ethnology
3. Appreciate how anthropologists conduct their research and the limits on such research:
   • ethnography
   • cross-cultural comparison
   • participant observation
4. Understand anthropology's relationship to the "hard sciences" and to the humanities:
   • the hypothesis-testing framework
5. Think about some of the ethical issues that confront anthropologists today.

Key Terms

anthropology

physical anthropology

cultural anthropology

forensic anthropology

culture-bound

archaeology

linguistic anthropology

ethnology

ethnography

participant observation

holistic perspective

hypothesis

theory

ethnohistory

cultural deprivation

forensic anthropology

Review Questions

1. What are the four subfields of anthropology? How are they related to each other?

2. How does Haviland define "culture?"

3. Distinguish between ethnology and ethnography.

4. Explain in what sense anthropology is a relatively recent product of Western civilization.

5. How does anthropology use the research of many other disciplines?

6. Why are anthropology and sociology closely allied? What sets them apart?

7. Cultural adaptation, development, and evolution are three general concerns of anthropologists. How are they interrelated?

8. Why do archaeologists excavate sites from the historical period when many documents provide information on recent culture?

9. What is the significance of "The Garbage Project?"

10. Why did archaeologists have difficulty in interpreting remains of large Mayan settlements in Central America?

11. With what aspects of language are linguists concerned?

12. How do linguists aid in our study of the past?

13. Describe the role of the ethnologist, giving an example of the sort of study an ethnologist would produce.

14. What is participant-observation? What are its advantages and disadvantages when compared to other social science methods?

15. Define "ethnohistory" and discuss its contributions to historical and ethnographic understanding.

16. Why might it be advisable to do research outside one's own culture prior to studying one's own?

17. What is meant by cross-cultural comparison? What significance does it have?

18. What is "total biography" as described by the anthropologist in Truk?

19. How did the anthropologist on Truk rule out various explanations of the attack on the truck in which he was riding shortly after his arrival in Truk?

20. How did anthropologist Philleo Nash affect the policies of the Roosevelt and Truman administrations?

21. What are the two key elements in the derivation of scientific laws, according to Haviland?

22. Explain the "self-correcting" nature of science, and give an example.

23. What are the limitations of the scientific approach, according to Haviland?

24. What problems are encountered when using the questionnaire for information gathering in ethnographic research?

25. How was anthropologist Sean Collins able to aid in the understanding of exchange relations in rural Peru?

26. What might be accomplished by research into one particular culture?

27. What distinguishes anthropology from the "hard sciences"?

28. Why must anthropologists exercise caution prior to publishing the results of their research?

29. To whom are anthropologists ultimately responsible?

30. How did Laura Nader explain her ethical position with regard to her work on the Zapotec and on U.S. energy research?

31. What is meant by a "global community"?

Fill-in-the-Blank

1. Anthropology is the study of _____ everywhere, throughout time.

2. Anthropology is one of several disciplines in the social and natural sciences that study humans. It differs from other disciplines primarily in its ability to _____ data from many sources.

3. Anthropologists recognize that human behavior has both _____ and social/cultural aspects.

4. Anthropology is divided into four branches, one of _____ anthropology and three of _____ anthropology (archaeology, linguistics, and ethnology).

5. An example of a practical application of physical anthropology is _____ anthropology, in which anthropologists testify in legal situations concerning human skeletal remains.

6. Archaeology is the study of culture based on _____ remains.

7. An in-depth description of a specific culture is called an _____.

8. Comparisons of "housework" shows that _____ spend less time on household tasks than Westerners do with all their time-saving gadgets.

9. A tentative explanation of the relation between certain phenomena (e.g., "The light failed to work because the filament was broken") is called a _____.

10. When archaeologists studied the Classic period of Maya civilization, they assumed that tropical forests occupied by people practicing _____ could not support large population clusters.

11. Ethnohistory is the study of cultures of the recent past through analysis of _____ materials.

12. Anthropological research is just as likely to be funded by the National Science Foundation as it is by the National Endowment for the _____.

Multiple-Choice Practice Questions

1. Anthropology is

a. the study of Western culture primarily through the analysis of its folklore.
b. the study of humankind everywhere, throughout time.
c. the study of only nonhuman primates through behavioral analysis.
d. the study of the species Homo sapiens by analyzing its biological but not its cultural dimensions.
e. the analysis of humankind from the subjective perspective of one group.

2. Anthropology developed as Europeans shifted from the use of biblical mythology to explanations based on

a. myth.
b. folklore.
c. hearsay.
d. natural laws.
e. gossip.

3. Anthropology differs from other disciplines that study humans in its ability to _____ data from many sources.

a. synthesize
b. eliminate
c. invent
d. falsify
e. fabricate

4. Anthropology is traditionally divided into four branches, one of _____ anthropology and three of _____ anthropology.

a. cultural/physical
b. physical/cultural
c. archaeological/linguistic
d. ethnological/physical
e. biological/physical

5. As part of your job, you may study the frequency of blood types in human populations, watch the behavior of monkeys and apes, or dig for early hominid bones in East Africa. You are a/an

a. ethnologist.
b. primatologist.
c. ethologist.
d. physical anthropologist.
e. cultural anthropologist.

6. A "culture-bound" theory is

a. a prediction that is bound to be fulfilled in a particular culture.
b. a theory developed by a cultural anthropologist rather than a physical anthropologist.
c. a theory developed by a sociologist rather than a cultural anthropologist.
d. a theory based on assumptions common to a particular culture rather than deriving from comparisons of many different cultures.
e. a theory based on comparison of cultures.

7. An archaeologist might attempt to

a. study material remains to reconstruct past cultures.
b. study present languages to reconstruct when they diverged from a parent stock.
c. study garbage to explain contemporary behavior.
d. all of the above
e. *a* and *c*

8. _____ is that branch of anthropology concerned with humans as biological organisms.

a. Archaeology
b. Cultural anthropology
c. Ethnology
d. Physical anthropology
e. Paleontology

9. In-depth descriptive studies of specific cultures are called

a. ethnologies.
b. ethnobotanies.
c. biologies.
d. ethnographies.
e. anthropologies.

10. Anthropologists doing fieldwork typically involve themselves in many different experiences. They try to investigate not just one aspect of culture (such as the political system) but how all aspects relate to each other (for example, how the political system fits with economic institutions, religious beliefs, etc.). This approach is called the _____ perspective.

a. holistic
b. ethnological
c. sociocultural
d. sociological
e. culture-bound

11. Ethnographic fieldwork

a. is usually associated with the study of wealthy elites.
b. is usually associated with the study of North American society.
c. is usually associated with the study of non-Western peoples.
d. can be applied, with useful results, to the study of North American peoples.
e. *c* and *d*

12. Ethnographic research on the cultural deprivation theories of the 1960s helped to demonstrate that

a. minority children are culturally deprived.
b. cultural deprivation causes lack of achievement in minority children.
c. the theory that minority children fail to achieve because they are culturally deprived is true.
d. the theory that minority children fail to achieve because they are culturally deprived is a culture-bound theory.
e. all of the above except *d*

13. Besides being interested in descriptions of particular cultures, the ethnologist is interested in

a. destroying particular cultures to improve them.
b. cross-cultural comparisons.
c. descriptions of nonhuman societies.
d. promoting Western ways.
e. teaching food foragers how to use timesaving gadgets.

14. The goal of science is

a. to discover the universal principles that govern the workings of the visible world.
b. to develop explanations of the world that are testable and correctable.
c. to eliminate the need to use the imagination.
d. all of the above
e. *a* and *b*

15. Archaeologists studying the Classic period of Mayan civilization before about 1960 made culture-bound assumptions that the Classic Maya

a. were more developed than present populations in their forms of agriculture.
b. were food foragers.
c. practiced the same slash-and-burn cultivation that people do today, and therefore could not have lived in large, permanent settlements.
d. lived in large, permanent settlements based on slash-and-burn cultivation.
e. were industrialists with space-age technology.

16. Questionnaire surveys

a. enable anthropologists to discover unexpected patterns of behavior.
b. are never used by anthropologists.
c. are used by anthropologists to supplement information gained by some other means.
d. are used only by sociologists.
e. get at real (vs. ideal) patterns of behavior.

17. Ideally, on which of the following are theories in cultural anthropology based?

a. intensive fieldwork done in a single society
b. ethnographies from all over the world so that statements made about culture will be universally applicable
c. worldwide questionnaire surveys
d. intuitive thinking about society and culture based on experiences in one's own society
e. the theories about culture formulated by the people one has studied

18. _____ refers to the study of cultures of the recent past through accounts left by explorers, missionaries, and traders, and through analysis of archival materials.

a. Social change
b. Ethnohistory
c. Cross-cultural comparison
d. Science
e. Formulation of hypotheses

19. Anthropology studies the language of a culture, its philosophy, and its forms of art. In the process of doing research, ethnographers involve themselves intensively in the lives of those they study, trying to experience culture from their informants' points of view. In this sense, anthropology is

a. scientific.
b. humanistic.
c. radical.
d. conservative.
e. systematic.

20. The anthropologist has to consider obligations to three sets of people:

a. the anthropologist's family, the host government, and the people studied.
b. the people who funded the study, the anthropologist's government, and the people studied.
c. the profession of anthropology, other anthropologists who have studied the community, and the community studied.
d. the anthropologist's students, parents, and the people studied.
e. the profession of anthropology, the people who funded the study, and the people studied.

21. Linguistic anthropology is concerned with

a. the description of language.
b. the history of language.
c. how language reflects a people's understanding of the world around them.
d. *a* and *b*
e. *a, b,* and *c*

Answers to multiple-choice practice questions

1. b   2. d   3. a   4. b   5. d   6. d   7. e   8. a   9. d   10. a   11. e   12. d   13. b
14. c   15. c   16. c   17. b   18. b   19. b   20. e   21. e

True/False Practice Questions

1. Culture is preserved and transmitted by language.

2. While ethnography is the in-depth study of a single culture, ethnology is the comparative study of culture.

3. Ethnographic fieldwork is never done in Western societies.

4. Anthropology can best be defined as the cross-cultural study of social behavior.

5. Forensic anthropologists are particularly interested in the use of anthropological information for purposes of debate, oratory and rhetorical criticism.

6. The anthropologist who went to Truk for his fieldwork was killed by a drunken Truk man.

Answers to true/false practice questions

1. T   2. T   3. F   4. F   5. F   6. F

Practice Matching

Match the anthropologist with his or her work.

1. _____ Clyde Snow   a. Wrote a popular introductory textbook

2. _____ William Haviland   b. Used forensic anthropology to investigate South American "disappearances"

3. _____ Laura Nader   c. Advised the Roosevelt and Truman administrations

4. _____ Philleo Nash   d. Confronted ethical problems in studying U.S. energy issues

5. _____ Sean Conlin   e. Found out that people in rural Peru didn't behave as their questionnaire responses indicated

Answers to practice matching

1. b   2. a   3. d   4. c   5. e

Practice Essays

1. Ilustrate the usefulness of ethnographic fieldwork in North American society by discussing research on the theory of cultural deprivation among minority children.

2. Discuss the characteristics of participation-observation and how this method contributes to ethnographic understanding. How is this method characteristically different from other methods of social science research?

3. Is anthropology one of the sciences or one of the humanities? In what ways does it contain elements of both?

4. According to the professional code of ethics of the American Anthropological Association, an anthropologist's primary responsibility is to the people he or she studies. Discuss the ethical issues that might arise where there is a conflict of interest between the scholar's commitment to "truth" and his or her commitment to people.

5. Haviland asserts that anthropology is a kind of testing ground for the cross-cultural validity of disciplines like sociology, psychology, and economics, saying that it is to these disciplines what the laboratory is to physics and chemistry. What theory in another social science discipline can you think of that could usefully be tested cross-culturally?

6. Discuss how the anthropologist in Truk used his experiences with drunken people to explain the cultural dynamics of the society.

Chapter 2
The Nature of Culture

Synopsis

In Chapter 2 the author considers the concept of culture, which underlies the anthropological enterprise. He proposes possible avenues for the definition of culture and describes how anthropologists attempt to study culture in the field. Finally, he raises questions as to whether it is possible for anthropologists to evaluate and compare cultures.

What You Should Learn from This Chapter

1. Understand what culture is.
2. Know how culture is transmitted along generations.
3. Know how anthropologists conduct research into cultures.
4. Understand how culture functions in society.
5. Understand the relationship between culture and adaptation.

Key Terms and Names

culture

society

social structure

gender

subcultures

pluralistic societies

enculturation

Leslie White

A.R. Radcliffe-Brown

integration

adaptation

Bronislaw Malinowski

ethnocentrism

cultural relativism

structural-functionalism

cultural materialism

symbol

Review Questions

1. What are four characteristics of culture, according to Haviland?

2. Distinguish between "culture" and "society." Do they always go together?

3. Distinguish between sex and gender.

4. Give an example of a pluralistic society, and consider what factors seem to allow the larger culture to tolerate subcultural variation.

5. How is culture passed on?

6. What is meant by the "integration" of the various aspects of culture? Give an example.

7. How was anthropology able to contribute to the architectural problems of the Apache Indians?

8. What are three ways in which anthropologists should obtain data in another culture, according to the text?

9. How did Malinowski define the "needs" to be fulfilled by all cultures?

10. What did Annette Weiner find out about Trobriand women?

11. How do the Yanomami adapt to their sociopolitical environment?

12. What five functions must a culture serve, according to your text?

13. What changes have recently impacted many pastoralists in sub-Saharan Africa?

14. In what ways must a balance be struck between society and the individuals who comprise it?

15. How can the large-scale sacrifices of the Aztec be explained?

16. Distinguish between ethnocentrism and cultural relativism.

17. What aspects of society indicate how well the physical and psychological needs of its people are being met, according to Walter Goldschmidt?

18. What was E.B. Tylor's original definition of culture in 1871? (This is a classic definition in anthropology, so it would be worthwhile to become familiar with it.)

19. Approximately how old is human culture?

Fill-in-the-Blank

1. The culture concept was first developed in the _____ century.

2. Haviland defines culture as "a set of _____ shared by members of a society that when acted upon by the members of a society, produce behavior that falls within a range of variance the members consider proper and acceptable."

3. When groups function within a society with their own distinctive standards of behavior, we speak of _____ variation.

4. Enculturation refers to the process through which culture is transmitted from one _____ to the next.

5. According to anthropologist _____, all human behavior originates in the use of symbols.

6. Radcliffe-Brown was the originator of a school of thought known as _____.

7. In Kapauku culture, gardens of _____ supply most of the food, but it is through breeding pigs that a man achieves political power.

8. There is a difference between what people say the rules are and actual behavior; that is, the anthropologist must distinguish between the _____ and the real.

9. Inheritance among the Trobrianders is carried through the _____ line.

10. Most organisms adapt by acquiring changes in their _____.

11. Pastoral nomadic people in Africa south of the _____ have survived droughts because of their mobility.

12. The members of all societies consider their own culture to be the best; thus all people can be said to be _____.

13. Anthropology tries to promote cultural _____, or the idea that a culture must be evaluated according to its own standards.

Exercise

Briefly identify the cultures listed below and locate them on the world map.

1. Amish   2. Kapauku Papuans

3. Trobrianders   4. Apache

Multiple-Choice Practice Questions

1. Culture, defined today, has changed from the meaning given to it during the nineteenth century. Today,

a. culture is seen as values and beliefs that lie behind behavior rather than as actual behavior.
b. culture is seen as real rather than as ideal.
c. the term "culture" has been replaced by the term "society."
d. culture is defined as objects rather than ideas.
e. the term "culture" is not used.

2. People share the same culture if they

a. are dependent on each other for survival.
b. are able to interpret and predict each other's actions.
c. live in the same territory.
d. behave in an identical manner.
e. all of the above

3. Which of the following statements about society and culture is INCORRECT?

a. Culture can exist without a society.
b. A society can exist without culture.
c. Ants and bees have societies but no culture.
d. A culture is shared by the members of a society.
e. Although members of a society may share a culture, their behavior is not uniform.

4. Every culture teaches its members that there are differences between people based on sex, age, occupation, class, and ethnic group. People learn to predict the behavior of people playing different roles from their own. This means that

a. culture is shared even though everyone is not the same.
b. everyone plays the same role.
c. all cultures identify the same roles.
d. all cultures require that their participants play different roles, even though that means that no one can predict the behavior of others.
e. everyone plays the same role throughout his or her life.

5. The cultural definitions of what it means to be a male or female today

a. are determined by biological differences.
b. are independent of biological differences.
c. stem from biological differences that today are relatively insignificant.
d. developed about 60 million years ago.
e. have no relationship to sex.

6. When groups function within a society with their own distinctive standards of behavior, we speak of

a. subcultural variation.
b. social structure.
c. gender differences.
d. cultural materialism.
e. ethnocentrism.

7. The Amish may be used as an example of a/an

a. pluralistic society.
b. subculture.
c. integrated society.
d. world culture.
e. complex society.

8. The process by which culture is transmitted from one generation to the next is

a. enculturation.
b. pluralism.
c. adaptation.
d. cultural relativism.
e. subcultural variation.

9. Which of the following statements is INCORRECT?

a. All culture is learned.
b. All learned behavior is cultural.
c. Culture is humankind's "social heredity."
d. Culture is not biologically inherited.
e. The process whereby culture is transmitted from one generation to the next is called enculturation.

10. The most important symbolic aspect of culture is

a. art.
b. language.
c. religion.
d. money.
e. politics.

11. Among the Kapauku Papuans of New Guinea, the fact that an attempt to eliminate warfare (which would create a balanced sex ratio) would affect the practice of polygyny, which would affect the economy (since women raise pigs, and the more wives a man has the more pigs he can keep), shows that culture is

a. materialistic.
b. relative.
c. pluralistic.
d. integrated.
e. enculturated.

12. An anthropologist develops a concept of culture by considering which of the following sources of data from the field?

a. what people say they ought to do
b. how people think they are behaving in accordance with these rules
c. what people actually do
d. all of the above
e. none of the above

13. When Annette Weiner went to the Trobriand Islands sixty years after Malinowski had been there, she found that

a. the culture had changed so much that it was almost unrecognizable.
b. Malinowski's views of wealth, political power, and descent were primarily from the male's point of view.
c. Malinowski had attributed power to women that did not exist.
d. only women were significant producers of wealth.
e. women played no role in producing wealth.

14. The process by which organisms adjust beneficially to their environment, or the characteristics by which they overcome hazards and gain access to the resources they need to survive, is called

a. culture.
b. biology.
c. social structure.
d. integration.
e. adaptation.

15. Behavior can be adaptive in the short run but maladaptive in the long run. In the Central Valley in California, vast irrigation projects have created a garden, but salts and chemicals accumulating in the soil will eventually create another desert. This same process occurred in

a. Mexico.
b. Morocco.
c. ancient Mesopotamia.
d. Great Britain.
e. the Yellow River valley of China.

16. A culture must satisfy basic needs such as

a. the distribution of necessary goods and services.
b. biological continuity through reproduction and enculturation of functioning adults.
c. maintenance of order within a society and between a society and outsiders.
d. motivation to survive.
e. all of the above

17. According to Leslie White, which of the following is a symbol?

a. a painting
b. a novel
c. walking across an intersection
d. brushing your teeth
e. all of the above

18. _____ refers to the position that because cultures are unique, each one can be evaluated only according to its own standards and values.

a. Ethnocentrism
b. Cultural relativism
c. Cultural materialism
d. Adaptation
e. Pluralism

19. Goldschmidt suggests that it is possible to decide which cultures are more successful than others by looking at which ones

a. survive.
b. last the longest.
c. satisfy the physical and cultural needs of the people.
d. support the most people.
e. are the least emotional.

Answers to multiple-choice practice questions

1. a   2. b   3. a   4. a   5. c   6. a   7. b   8. a   9. b   10. b   11. d   12. d
13. b   14. e   15. c   16. e   17. e   18. b   19. c

True/False Practice Questions

1. To say that culture is shared means that all members of a society behave in the same way.

2. A pluralistic society always has subcultural variation, but not every society with subcultural variation is pluralistic.

3. A larger culture is more likely to tolerate a subculture if their values and physical appearances are similar.

4. Cattle herding is the mainstay around which all of Kapauku Papuan society revolves.

5. A modern definition of culture emphasizes the values, beliefs, and rules that lie behind behavior rather than the actual observable behavior itself.

6. Gender differences were more extreme among food foragers than among late nineteenth and early twentieth century Westerners.

7. Annette Weiner agrees that ethnographic writing can never be more than a fictional account.

8. There are some societies that have no regulation of sex whatsoever.

Answers to true/false practice questions

1. F   2. T   3. T   4. F   5. T   6. F   7. F   8. F

Practice Matching

Match the culture with its description.

1. _____ Amish

    a. A Native American people with distinct architectural needs

2. _____ Trobrianders

    b. A Pacific Island people studied by both Malinowski and Weiner

3. _____ Kapauku Papuans

    c. A pacifist agrarian subculture of the U.S.

4. _____ Aztec

    d. A New Guinea people who breed pigs

5. _____ Apache

    e. A civilization in Mexico which engaged in large-scale sacrifices

Answers to practice matching

1. c   2. b   3. d   4. e   5. a

Practice Essays

1. Using the Amish as an example of subcultural variation, discuss some of the factors that seem to determine whether or not subcultural variation is tolerated by the larger culture. Compare the Amish to another group that is less well-tolerated.

2. Using the example of the Kapauku Papuans, explain the idea that culture is integrated. Illustrate the notion of the integration of culture with another culture, comparing it with Kapauku Papuans as you do so.

3. Anthropologist James Peacock wrote a book called *The Anthropological Lens* in which he compared culture to a lens or glass through which people experience the world. The anthropologist, then, is like an oculist who hopes to find the "formula" of each kind of lens, acquiring a kind of stereoscopy, or depth perception, by being able to perceive things through multiple lenses. How is culture like a lens? What are the limitations of this metaphor for understanding culture and anthropology?

4. Are animals other than humans capable of culture?

Chapter 3
The Beginnings of Human Culture

Synopsis

Culture evolved as the primary adaptation of our species over millions of years. In this chapter Haviland traces the intertwining of biological and cultural evolution through the history of our fossil ancestors, looking at major milestones like the development of stone tools, the first use of fire, the rise of cooperative hunting, and language as a means of communication.

What You Should Learn from This Chapter

1. Understand that culture is our species' major mode of adaptation.
2. Know the major fossil ancestors of our species and approximately where and when they lived.
3. Understand the biological changes that led to the current physical structure of our species.
4. Know what the major milestones in the development of culture were, and approximately where and when they occurred.
5. Understand how the study of human evolution complements and enhances the study of the diversity of cultures today.

Key Terms and Names

primate order

natural selection

Jane Goodall

sivapithecines

Australopithecus

hominine

Homo habilis

Oldowan tools

Paleolithic

Homo erectus

Homo sapiens

Neandertals

Mousterian tools

Upper Paleolithic

Review Questions

1. To what biological order do humans belong? What other kinds of animals belong to
   this order?

2. Describe the environment to which early primates adapted through natural selection.

3. What are the distinguishing features of the primates?

4. In what ways can apes adapt to their environment through learning?

5. Why was Project Washoe a major step in the understanding of chimpanzee cognition?

6. What is the evidence that the sivapithecines are likely human ancestors?

7. Why is dentition important to the study of human evolution?

8. Under what conditions might bipedalism have emerged?

9. What features of *Australopithecus* were more humanlike, and what features were more apelike?

10. What are the fossil species into which *Australopithecus* is divided? Identify each.

11. What was the "protein problem" faced by evolving primates? How was it resolved?

12. When and where did the first stone tools appear? What were they like?

13. How did the appearance of stone tools relate to changes in brain size, teeth, and diet?

14. How did the different roles played by males and females in the search for food affect selection for intelligence in early *Homo*?

15. What was the geographical distribution of *Homo erectus*? What were its physical characteristics?

16. What was the impact of the use of fire on our fossil ancestors?

17. What other cultural developments took place during *Homo erectus* times?

18. What is the difference between a hominine and a hominid?

19. What is the role played by grooming in primate social order?

20. When did *Homo sapiens* first appear? What were its characteristics?

21. What is the "Eve hypothesis?" What is the evidence for and against it?

22. What was the tool-making tradition of the Neandertals?

23. In what other ways did culture develop in Neandertal times?

24. What were the major cultural developments of the Upper Paleolithic?

Fill-in-the-Blank

1. Humans belong to the _____ Order, along with lemurs, indriids, lorises, tarsiers, monkeys, and apes.

2. Primates have fewer and less _____ teeth in comparison to the ancestral animals from which they evolved.

3. The senses that are highly developed in primates are _____, touch, and smell.

4. The tree-dwelling environment to which early primates adapted is called an _____ habitat.

5. The depth perception characteristic of primates stems from their _____ vision.

6. Instead of claws, most primates have _____.

7. Primate brains are large, especially the _____ hemispheres.

8. A behavior of primates that encourages social bonding is _____.

9. Jane Goodall carried out a long-term study of chimpanzees in _____.

10. Washoe learned to recognize herself in a mirror, suggesting that chimps have brains that can formulate a _____.

11. The sivapithecines lived about _____ million years ago.

12. Some features of sivapithecines resemble an Asian ape called an _____.

13. The first hominine to walk fully upright was _____.

14. Walking on two legs is called _____.

15. A new find that may represent the earliest form of *Australopithecus* is _____.

16. The earliest stone tools are about _____ million years old.

17. It was *Homo* _____ who made Oldowan tools.

18. *Homo erectus* spread beyond Africa to _____.

19. Neandertal tool-making traditions are called _____.

20. The _____ hypothesis suggests that all modern humans are derived from a single population of archaic *H. sapiens*.

21. Upper Paleolithic peoples spread into two new geographic areas: _____ and _____.

Exercises

I. Map

On the world map below, mark the approximate ranges of the following fossil forms (make a key so that you can use this to study from).

a. sivapithecines
b. *Australopithecus*
c. *Homo habilis*
d. *Homo erectus*
e. *Homo sapiens*

II. Comparative Skeletal Structure

Below are skeletons of a chimpanzee and a modern human being. Discuss the major anatomical differences between them, pointing out what selective pressures might be responsible. (Using colors to mark similar structures may help make this clearer for review purposes.)

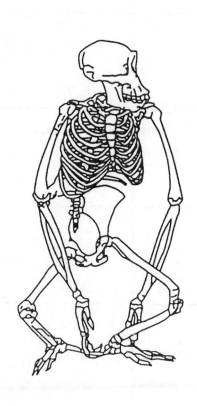

III. Complete the following chart to use as a study aid in reviewing human evolution.

Fossil Form	Dates	Range	Characteristics	Cultural Developments
sivapithecines				
Australopithecus				
Homo habilis				
Homo erectus				
Neandertals				
Upper Paleolithic *Homo sapiens*				

Multiple-Choice Practice Questions

1. The primate order includes which of the following types of animals?

    a. tarsiers
    b. lorises
    c. indriids
    d. all of the above
    e. none of the above

2. Which of the following characteristics distinguishes primates from other mammals?

    a. a large complex brain in which the area devoted to smell is quite large
    b. the development of more teeth of a highly specialized nature
    c. increased visual acuity because of stereoscopic and color vision
    d. the development of a specific breeding season and increased number of offspring
    e. all of the above

3. The case of Washoe, the chimpanzee, showed that

    a. chimps have intelligence similar to humans, at least when they are young.
    b. some chimps can actually learn to talk.
    c. chimps have a culture just as humans do.
    d. chimps have conceptual capabilities far beyond what had previously been suspected.
    e. the scientific community could be unanimous in its enthusiastic reception of an
        important project.

4. The transition to bipedalism probably occurred in a context where primates spent a lot
    of time in the trees but ventured out periodically onto the open savanna to exploit the
    food resources there. This transition occurred because bipedalism conferred the
    advantage of

    a. being able to climb trees more effectively.
    b. being able to run faster on the ground.
    c. freeing the hands for a variety of purposes.
    d. all of the above
    e. none of the above

5. *Australopithecus* was more like an ape than a human in its

    a. teeth.
    b. jaws.
    c. brain-body ratio.
    d. posture and form of locomotion.
    e. all of the above

6. The earliest known tool tradition

a. is called Oldowan.
b. begins about 2 million years ago.
c. marks the beginning of the Paleolithic.
d. all of the above
e. none of the above

7. Which form had a geographic range of Africa, Southeast Asia, Europe, and China?

a. *Australopithecus*
b. the sivapithecines
c. *Homo erectus*
d. Neandertal
e. *Homo sapiens*

8. These people developed an extensive art and decorative tradition.

a. *Homo habilis*
b. *Homo erectus*
c. Neandertal
d. Upper Paleolithic
e. fully modern *Homo sapiens*

9. Jane Goodall is highly respected for her work with

a. chimpanzees.
b. gorillas.
c. orangutans.
d. macaques.
e. lorises.

Answers to multiple-choice practice questions

1. d   2. c   3. d   4. d   5. c   6. d   7. c   8. d   9. a

True/False Practice Questions

1. The environment selected for the distinctive characteristics of the primate order was arboreal.

2. Chimpanzees have been observed to hunt cooperatively and to share meat.

3. *Homo habilis* learned how to use fire at the same time as it developed Oldowan tools.

4. Hominines became bipedal at about the same time as their brain size radically increased.

5. There is some dispute about the relationship between the Neandertals and ourselves.

Answers to true/false practice questions

1. T   2. T   3. F   4. F   5. T

Practice Matching

1. _____ *Homo habilis*   a. Learned to use fire

2. _____ *Homo erectus*   b. First biped

3. _____ *Australopithecus*   c. First stone tool maker

4. _____ sivapithecines   d. Spread to Australia and the
                                               Americas

5. _____ *Homo sapiens*   e. A human-ape ancestor

Answers to practice matching

1. c   2. a   3. b   4. e   5. d

Practice Essays

1. If you had to pick three to six key developments in the evolution of culture, what would they be? Write an essay identifying their importance to culture as we know among human beings.

2. What one question do you feel remains unanswered about the evolution of humans and human culture? That is, if you could make one key discovery, what would it be? Why would it be critical to our understanding of evolution?

Chapter 4
Language and Communication

Synopsis

Chapter 4 introduces the field of anthropological linguistics, considering how existing languages are described and studied and what the history of language can tell us. It examines how language is related to culture and explores the evolution of the capacity for language. An extensive technical vocabulary relating to linguistics is presented.

What You Should Learn from This Chapter

1. Know how humans communicate with one another.
2. Know what linguistics is and the components of language.
3. Understand how humans use paralanguage to communicate.
4. Understand how humans use kinesics to communicate.
5. Know how ethnolinguistics aids in understanding culture.
6. Know the explanations offered about the origin of language.

Key Terms

language

symbol

signal

linguistics

phonetics

phonology

phonemes

morphemes

bound morpheme

free morpheme

frame substitution

syntax

grammar

form classes

kinesics

paralanguage

voice qualities

vocalizations

vocal characterizers

vocal qualifiers

vocal segregates

language family

linguistic divergence

glottochronology

core vocabulary

linguistic nationalism

ethnolinguistics

Sapir-Whorf hypothesis

dialects

sociolinguistics

code switching

displacement

Review Questions

1. Why is language so important to culture?

2. What is the anatomical "price we pay" for our vocal capabilities?

3. What does primatologist Allison Jolly mean by the "audience effect" she observes among the primates she studies?

4. Distinguish between a morpheme and a phoneme and give an example of each.

5. Distinguish between bound and free morphemes, and give examples of each.

6. What is the function of frame substitution?

7. What is the purpose of a form class?

8. What method does descriptive linguistics use?

9. What is paralanguage? Provide examples.

10. What are the characteristic differences in body posture between men and women?

11. What is the "gesture-call" system?

12. What are the elements of voice quality?

13. Distinguish between vocal characterizers and vocal qualifiers.

14. How are gender markers employed?

15. What is code switching? Give an example you have observed.

16. What does glottochronology seek to explain?

17. Describe the importance of language for group identity.

18. What does ethnolinguistics seek to explain?

19. Provide an example that would support the Sapir-Whorf hypothesis.

20. What is meant by color-naming behavior?

21. How can linguists use metaphor as a key to understanding culture?

22. Why do linguists study kinship terms?

23. Haviland notes that wild speculation about the origins of language is no longer necessary. What advances have been made that make such speculation unnecessary?

24. What types of communication have primates been taught?

25. What are the communicative capabilities of monkeys and apes?

26. What is the difference between a signal and a symbol?

Fill-in-the-Blank

1. There are about _____ languages in the world.

2. A symbol has an arbitrary meaning determined by cultural convention, while a _____ has a natural or self-evident meaning.

3. Of all the potential sounds that can be made by the human vocal system, no more than _____ are used by any particular language.

4. The modern scientific study of language by Europeans began in the _____ with the collection of information about exotic languages by European explorers, invaders, and missionaries.

5. _____ is the systematic study of the production, transmission, and reception of speech sounds.

6. The smallest class of sound that makes a difference in meaning is called a _____.

7. The smallest significant unit of sound that carries a meaning is called a _____.

8. The entire formal structure of a language is called its _____.

9. The method used to define the rules and regularities of a language is called frame _____.

10. _____ refers to the extralinguistic noises that accompany language.

11. Voice _____ are the background characteristics of a speaker's voice that convey the state of the speaker.

12. Sounds such as "shh" and "uh-huh" that are similar to speech sounds but do not appear in sequences that can be called words are vocal _____.

13. _____ is usually referred to as "body language."

14. _____ linguistics studies relationships between earlier and later languages.

15. English belongs to the _____ language family.

16. Linguistic _____ refers to the attempt by nations to proclaim their independence and distinctive identity by celebrating their own language.

17. The study of the relationship between language and social factors is called _____.

18. The process by which a person changes from one level of language to another is called _____.

Multiple-Choice Practice Questions

1. A system of communication based on symbols is called a

a. signal.
b. form class.
c. language.
d. frame substitution.
e. vocalization.

2. All languages are organized on the same basic plan in that

a. they are all based on signals.
b. they take no more than fifty sounds and put them together in meaningful ways according to rules that can be determined by linguists.
c. they take no more than three thousand sounds and organize them according to the rules of grammar.
d. they all evolved from a common Egyptian language.
e. they originated in Russia.

3. The modern scientific study of all aspects of language is

a. kinesics.
b. phonology.
c. linguistics.
d. grammar.
e. glottochronology.

4. The systematic study of the production, transmission, and reception of speech sounds is

a. linguistics.
b. morphology.
c. frame substitution.
d. phonetics.
e. syntax.

5. Paralanguage is to speech as _____ is to position of the body.

a. kinesics
b. ethnolinguistics
c. form class
d. phonetics
e. displacement

6. Consider the English word "dog." Which of the following is a morpheme?

a. "d"
b. "dog"
c. "o"
d. "g"
e. all of the above

7. Variants of a single morpheme are called _____; for example, the sounds *s* and *z* in "cats" and "dogs."

a. allophones
b. allomorphs
c. free morphemes
d. bound morphemes
e. signals

8. The method called frame substitution enables the linguist to establish the rules or principles by which language users construct phrases and sentences, that is, the _____ of the language.

a. morphology
b. form classes
c. core vocabulary
d. sociolinguistics
e. syntax

9. Two people say to you, "You sure look nice today." Although they are saying the same words, you can tell that one person is being complimentary and the other sarcastic by their

a. vocalizations.
b. vocal characteristics.
c. voice qualities.
d. voice segregates.
e. vocal qualifiers.

10. Kinesics is a system for communication through

a. screaming.
b. kissing.
c. motion.
d. fighting.
e. food.

11. Descriptive linguistics

a. attempts to explain the features of a particular language at one time in its history.
b. looks at languages as separate systems without considering how they might be related to each other.
c. attempts to construct a language's historical development.
d. investigates relationships between earlier and later forms of the same language.
e. *a* and *b* only

12. A language family is a group of languages that

a. all have the same core vocabulary.
b. are subordinate to a dominant language.
c. all have the same syntax.
d. use the same number of sounds.
e. are descended from a single ancestral language.

13. If the core vocabulary of two languages is compared by glottochronologists, it is thought possible to determine

a. if the two languages perceive reality in the same way.
b. if the two languages use the same syntax.
c. if they share the same allophones.
d. if they have a similar technology.
e. how long ago the languages separated from each other.

14. Which of the following statements about linguistic divergence is INCORRECT?

a. One force for linguistic change is borrowing by one language from another.
b. If languages were isolated from each other, there would be very little linguistic change.
c. New vocabulary emerges in a language due to a quest for novelty and the development of specialized vocabulary by groups.
d. Changes in pronunciation may emerge as markers of class boundary (e.g., upper class "U" vs. "non-U").
e. Dying languages may be revived in the name of linguistic nationalism.

15. Which of the following is NOT an example of linguistic nationalism?

a. You are a Spanish-speaking person in the United States and want your children to learn English, so that they can assimilate more completely into the society around them.
b. A national committee in France declares that certain widely used terms will no longer be allowed to appear in public print because they are not French.
c. You live in Scotland and are so alarmed by the rapid decline in the number of people speaking Gaelic that you start a school in which all subjects are taught in Gaelic.
d. The southern part of India declares itself a separate country called Tamiland (the land of the people who speak Tamil) in defiance of India's declaration of Hindi as the national language; people say they will die in defense of their "mother tongue."
e. A country previously colonized by the British passes a law requiring everyone to speak the native tongue; English is banned because of its association with colonial domination.

16. The influence of a person's class status on what pronunciation he/she uses; a speaker's choice of more complicated vocabulary and grammar when he/she is speaking to a professional audience; the influence of language on culture--all these are the concerns of

a. descriptive linguistics.
b. historical linguistics.
c. ethnolinguistics.
d. linguistic nationalism.
e. displacement.

17. Which of the following statements about the Sapir-Whorf hypothesis is INCORRECT?

a. It was first formulated by Edward Sapir and Benjamin Lee Whorf.
b. It may be briefly explained with the sentence, "Language determines the reality that speakers of the language perceive."
c. It may be briefly explained with the sentence, "Language reflects reality; it only mirrors what people perceive."
d. It is expressed in this example: If in a factory a metal drum is labeled "empty" (when in fact it is filled with flammable fumes), people will perceive it as empty and may do things with it that may create a fire hazard (such as storing it near a furnace); but if it is labeled "full" of gaseous fumes, people will perceive it as a fire hazard and treat it more carefully.
e. None of the above is incorrect.

18. The term _____ is usually used to refer to varying forms of a language that reflect particular regions or social classes and that are similar enough to be mutually intelligible.

a. dialect
b. language subgroup
c. language family
d. linguistic nationalism
e. Sapir-Whorf hypothesis

54

Answers to multiple-choice practice questions

1. c   2. b   3. c   4. d   5. a   6. b   7. b   8. e   9. c   10. c   11. e   12. e
13. e   14. b   15. a   16. c   17. c   18. a

True/False Practice Questions

1. Haviland traces linguistics back to the ancient grammarians in China more than three thousand years ago.

2. Glottochronology assumes that the rate at which a language's core vocabulary changes is variable and thus cannot be used to give an exact date for when two languages diverged.

3. According to the hypothesis devised by Sapir and Whorf, if you had only one word to describe what English speakers call "red" and "yellow," you would not be likely to perceive the shades of red and yellow in a sunset.

4. Though men and women in North American culture typically utilize slightly different vocabularies, the body language they use does not differ much.

5. The emphasis on the French language by Quebecois separatists is an example of linguistic nationalism.

Answers to true/false practice questions

1. T   2. F   3. T   4. F   5. T

Practice Matching

Match the term to its definition.

1. _____ bound morpheme

a. A method of dating divergence within language families

2. _____ phonemes

b. The smallest classes of sound that make a difference in meaning

3. _____ form classes

c. A sound that occurs in a language only in combination with other sounds, as *s* in English to signify the plural

4. _____ kinesics

d. Postures, facial expressions, and body motion

5. _____ glottochronology

e. The parts of speech that work the same way in any sentence

Answers to practice matching

1. c   2. b   3. e   4. d   5. a

Practice Essays

1. Would it be accurate to claim language as a distinguishing feature of *H. sapiens?* Why or why not? What evidence exists for the uniqueness or nonuniqueness of human language?

2. How is language linked to gender? Use examples from the text and add some of your own.

Chapter 5
Growing up Human

Synopsis

Chapter 5 focuses on how culture is transmitted from one generation to the next and explores the cultural contexts in which personalities are formed. It suggests a relativistic understanding of normality and abnormality and looks at recent changes in the field of psychological anthropology.

What You Should Learn from This Chapter

1. Understand the process and agents of enculturation.
2. Understand how the behavioral environment functions.
3. Understand how personality is shaped.
4. Understand the concepts of dependence and independence training in child rearing.
5. Know how group personality is determined.
6. Understand the purpose and criticisms of national character studies.
7. Know how normality and abnormality are defined.

Key Terms and Names

enculturation

self-awareness

patterns of affect

personality

Margaret Mead

dependence training

independence training

group personality

modal personality

national character

Ruth Fulton Benedict

core values

mental illness

ethnic psychoses

Review Questions

1. Who are the agents of enculturation?

2. What are three aspects of self-awareness, according to Haviland?

3. Why might North American children's motor development lag behind that of children from non-Western societies?

4. What are three aspects of the behavioral environment?

5. What does the study of the Penobscot tell us about culture and personality?

6. Describe the situaton of the Ju/'hoansi.

7. What did the Original Study of the Mbuti indicate about child-rearing patterns?

8. Distinguish between dependence and independence training.

9. What did Margaret Mead's study of adolescent Samoans tell us?

10. Provide an example of modal personality.

11. Explain the basic statistics behind the concept of modal personality.

12. What purpose do the Rorschach and Thematic Apperception Tests serve?

13. What does Francis Hsu suggest are major personality traits of the Chinese?

14. What problems accompany the use of modal personality assessment?

15. What contribution did Ruth Benedict make to the field of culture-and-personality?

16. Why were national character studies undertaken?

17. What was Gorer's toilet-training hypothesis?

18. What are the major objections to national character studies?

19. Provide examples of core values.

20. What is the function of the berdache in Plains Indians society?

21. How are male and female role identities shaped by the structure of the human family, according to Nancy Chodorow?

22. How is abnormal behavior defined?

23. How are cures effected among the Melemchi of Nepal?

24. What is "windigo?"

Fill-in-the-Blank

1. The Enlightenment thinker John Locke presented the concept of _____ to express the idea that humans are born as "blank slates" and that everything depends on experience.

2. The term _____ refers to the process by which culture is transmitted from one generation to the next.

3. The Penobscot traditionally conceived of the self as divided into two parts, the body and the _____.

4. Margart Mead studied three societies in _____ and found out that sex roles were highly variable.

5. Margaret Mead was a founder of the field called _____.

6. The Ju/'hoansi make a living by _____ in the Kalahari Desert.

7. A concept that attempted to retain the idea of a group personality and yet take into account the diversity of personalities within a group is the concept of _____.

8. The ink-blot test is properly called the _____ test.

9. The studies developed during World War II to explore the idea that modern nations could be characterized by personality types were called _____ studies.

10. The psychosis exhibited by northern Algonkian Indian groups who recognize the existence of cannibalistic monsters is called _____.

Exercise

Briefly identify the cultures listed below, and locate them on the world map.

1. Penobscot

2. Arapesh, Mundugamor, Tchambuli

3. Ju/'hoansi

4. Mbuti

5. Yanomami

6. Dobu

7. Melemchi

8. Algonkian Indians

Multiple-Choice Practice Questions

1. Enculturation is the process of transmitting

   a. society from one generation to the next.
   b. social norms from one adult to another.
   c. culture from one child to another.
   d. culture from one generation to the next.
   e. personality from parent to child.

2. The agents of enculturation

   a. are persons involved in transmitting culture to the next generation.
   b. are at first the members of the family into which the child is born.
   c. vary, depending on the structure of the family into which a child is born.
   d. include peer groups and schoolteachers.
   e. all of the above

3. Which of the following statements about self-awareness is INCORRECT?

   a. Self-awareness occurs earlier in children as a function of the amount of social stimulation they receive.
   b. At fifteen weeks of age, the home-reared infant in North America is in contact with its mother for about 20 percent of the time.
   c. At fifteen weeks of age, infants in the Ju/'hoansi society of South Africa's Kalahari Desert are in close contact with their mothers about 70 percent of the time.
   d. American children develop self-awareness earlier than do Ju/'hoansi children.
   e. all of the above are correct.

4. The _____ includes definitions and explanations of objects, spatial orientation, and temporal orientation, as well as culturally defined values, ideals, and standards that provide an individual with a normative orientation.

   a. vital self
   b. *tabula rasa*
   c. behavioral environment
   d. patterns of affect
   e. core values

5. In studying three societies in New Guinea, Margaret Mead found that the roles played by men and women were determined primarily by

a. genes.
b. biology.
c. culture.
d. incest.
e. the food they ate.

6. Margaret Mead's groundbreaking work in culture and personality published in 1928 was a deliberate test of a Western psychological hypothesis. What was this hypothesis?

a. Lowering the drinking age will promote promiscuity.
b. Child-rearing practices have no effect on adult personality.
c. The stress and conflict experienced by American adolescents is a universal phenomenon based on maturing hormones.
d. By changing child-rearing practices, we can change the structure of society.
e. By lowering the driving age, we can promote less stress among adolescents.

7. A study of child rearing among the Ju/'hoansi of Africa indicates that

a. boys and girls are raised in a very similar manner and are both mild-mannered and self-reliant.
b. because girls are out gathering most of the time, they are expected to be more aggressive and self-reliant than boys are.
c. mothers spend the least amount of time with their children, and thus the children identify strongly with their fathers.
d. boys do more work than girls.
e. boys have less responsibility than girls and get to play more of the time.

8. Independence training, according to Child and the Whitings, is more likely in

a. small nuclear families.
b. large extended families.
c. small-scale horticultural societies where a man has many wives.
d. a pastoralist family where a woman has many husbands and the extended family has to be always on the move.
e. New York City neighborhoods where large families stay nearby and support each other.

65

9. Dependence training is more likely in

a. nuclear families.
b. societies whose subsistence is based on pastoralism.
c. a food-foraging society.
d. extended families in societies whose economy is based on subsistence farming.
e. industrial societies.

10. The personality typical of a society, as indicated by the central tendency of a defined frequency distribution, is called

a. core values.
b. nuclear personality.
c. patterns of affect.
d. culture and personality.
e. modal personality.

11. Which of the following statements about modal personality is INCORRECT?

a. Although a modal personality may be found for a particular society, a range of personalities may exist in that society.
b. Although the modal personality may be considered "normal" for that society, it may be shared by less than half of the population.
c. Those who study modal personality accept the fact that there may be abnormal individuals in that society.
d. Data on modal personality are usually gathered by the use of psychological tests such as the Rorschach and TAT.
e. all of the above are correct.

12. Studies of _____ were developed during World War II to explore the idea that basic personality traits were shared by most of the people in modern nations.

a. modal personality
b. national character
c. stereotype
d. group personality
e. independence training

13. The term "core values" refers to

a. those aspects of culture that pertain to the way a culture makes its living.
b. rules that guide family and home life.
c. those values emphasized by a particular culture.
d. common shares in Golden Delicious Corp.
e. the beliefs of Oliver North.

14. Among the Plains Indians, a man who wore women's clothes, performed women's work, and married another man

a. was considered normal.
b. was sought out as a curer, artist, and matchmaker.
c. was assumed to have great spiritual power.
d. might have been homosexual.
e. all of the above

15. An ethnic psychosis refers to a

a. psychotic episode experienced by a person from an exotic culture.
b. progressive disease that strikes anthropologists when they spend more than twelve months in the field.
c. psychosis characterized by symptoms peculiar to a particular group.
d. universal form of mental illness.
e. biologically based disease that resembles schizophrenia.

16. Traditional culture and personality studies

a. were important in undermining ethnocentrism and promoting a relativistic point of view.
b. are criticized today for being impressionistic and difficult to replicate.
c. diversified the study of psychological processes in a cultural context.
d. *a, b,* and *c*
e. none of the above

17. Among the Yanomami

a. all men are fierce and warlike.
b. all men are quiet and retiring.
c. there is a range of personalities.
d. a quiet, retiring Yanomamo would not survive.
e. a fierce, warlike Yanomamo would not survive.

18. When Mbuti children enter the *bopi* or playground, the most important principle guiding their social interaction is their

a. gender.
b. age.
c. kinship relations.
d. class status.
e. caste status.

Answers to multiple-choice practice questions

1. d   2. e   3. d   4. c   5. c   6. c   7. a   8. a   9. d   10. e   11. e   12. b
13. c   14. e   15. c   16. d   17. c   18. b

True/False Practice Questions

1. What is considered "normal" in a society is defined by culture.

2. Anthropologists believe that all mental illness is learned rather than biologically based.

3. Both hunting and gathering societies and industrial societies promote independence training in their mobile nuclear families.

4. Margart Mead believed that male and female roles were by and large defined by the biological attributes of the sexes.

5. National character studies developed during World War II to explore the idea that basic personality traits were shared by most of the people in modern nations.

6. The primary contribution of Whiting and Child to the field of psychological anthropology was their in-depth study of the Ju/'hoansi.

7. The Yanomami of Brazil are known for their "fierceness," yet there is a range of personality types even there.

Answers to true/false practice questions

1. T   2. F   3. T   4. F   5. T   6. F   7. F

Practice Essays

1. Psychiatrist Thomas Szasz, in a book called *The Myth of Mental Illness*, described our society's medicalization of deviance, claiming that the decision to label a person as mentally ill is tied to the social, economic, and political order rather than to some absolute definition of sanity or normalcy. Is this an idea that anthropologists would be comfortable with? Can you compare this with any other examples of the social context of normality/abnormality discussed in the chapter?

2. What was the impact of Freudian psychoanalysis on the development of psychological anthropology? How have culture-and-personality specialists responded to the Freudian paradigm?

Chapter 6
Patterns of Subsistence

Synopsis

In Chapter 6 the text examines the impact that various modes of subsistence have on cultures. Food foraging is described in detail, and the variations in food production systems are discussed.

What You Should Learn from This Chapter

1. Understand the role of adaptation in cultural survival:
   - unit of adaptation
   - evolutionary adaptation
   - culture areas
   - culture core
2. Understand the food-foraging way of life:
   - subsistence and sex roles
   - food sharing
   - cultural adaptations and material technology
   - egalitarian society
3. Understand food-producing society:
   - horticulturalists
   - pastoralists
   - intensive agriculture and nonindustrial cities

Key Terms and Names

adaptation

horticulture

ecosystem

convergent evolution

71

parallel evolution

Julian Steward

culture area

culture type

cultural ecology

culture core

ethnoscientists

carrying capacity

density of social relations

pastoralist

swidden

preindustrial cities

Review Questions

1. What purpose does adaptation serve?

2. Describe the relationship the Tsembaga have with the environment.

3. Explain what is meant by a unit of adaptation.

4. What are human ecologists concerned with?

5. Describe Comanche adaptation to the plains environment.

6. Distinguish between convergent and parallel evolution.

7. Provide an example of how a culture can be stable while not necessarily static.

8. Use the Gururumba to illustrate horticulture as an adapative pattern of subsistence.

9. Why did native groups on the plains not farm?

10. What is the role of the ethnoscientist?

11. About how many people currently live by food foraging?

12. What previously held misconceptions of food foragers have been refuted?

13. What are the main social characteristics of food foragers?

14. What are the size-limiting factors in a foraging group?

15. What purpose does population redistribution serve for the Ju/'hoansi?

16. What impact does biological sex have on the division of labor?

17. How is the behavior of food-foraging groups reflected in their material culture?

18. Why are food foragers generally egalitarian?

19. Can we make any generalizations about the status of women in foraging societies?

20. How is territory conceptualized in foraging societies?

21. Define the concerns of Julian Steward's study of cultural ecology.

22. Distinguish between horticulturalists and intensive agriculturalists.

23. What are the basic features of pastoralist society?

24. Define "adaptation" and "ecosystem" and illustrate the relevance of these concepts with the example of pig sacrifices among the Tsembaga.

25. Why has slash-and-burn (swidden) come to be viewed negatively by many people today?

26. Describe the subsistence practices of the KeKranoti Kayapo.

27. How did anthropologist Alan Kolata help the Aymara with their agricultural problems?

Fill-in-the-Blank

1. _____ is the process by which organisms modify and adjust to their environment and thereby survive more effectively.

2. The main animal raised by the Gururumba is _____.

3. When the Comanche migrated to the Great Plains, they found a new food source, the _____.

4. When several societies with different cultural backgrounds move into a new environment and develop similar adaptations, they represent the cultural equivalent of _____ evolution.

5. When several societies with very similar cultural backgrounds develop along similar lines, they represent the process of _____ evolution.

6. A geographic region in which a number of different societies follow a similar pattern of life is called a culture _____.

7. The various societies of the Great Plains had common religious rituals, such as _____.

8. The subfield within anthropology that studies the interaction of specific cultures with their environments is called _____.

9. The anthropologist who pioneered this subfield was _____.

10. _____ try to understand folk ideologies and how they help a group survive.

11. Humans lived using food foraging until about _____ years ago, when domestication of animals and plants began.

12. The Ju/'hoansi of the Kalahari Desert have been called "the original _____ society" because they work so few hours a week.

13. The number of people who can be supported by a certain technology is the _____ of the environment.

14. About _____ percent of the diet of most food foragers is gathered by women.

15. Increased food sharing appears to be related to a shift in food habits involving increased eating of _____ around two and a half million years ago.

16. Another name for slash-and-burn is _____ farming.

17. The Bakhtiari of the Zagros Mountains are _____ who migrate seasonally from one location to another.

18. City life is based on a subsistence pattern of _____.

19. The main city of the Aztecs was _____.

20. The anthropologist who helped the Aymara was _____.

Exercises

I. Complete the chart below, filling in examples of each type of subsistence and noting its general characteristics. You can use this to study from later.

PATTERNS OF SUBSISTENCE

Type	Example	Characteristics
Foraging		
Pastoralism		
Horticulture		
Agriculture		

II. Briefly identify the cultures listed below, and locate them on the world map.

1. Tsembaga

2. Comanche

3. Shoshone and Paiute

4. Hadza

5. KeKranoti Kayapo

6. Gururumba

7. Bakhtiari

8. Aymara

Multiple-Choice Practice Questions

1. Adaptation refers to the

a. process by which organisms modify and adjust to their environment and thereby survive more effectively.
b. ability of one population to destroy another.
c. borrowing of cultural material from another society.
d. process by which living systems change from birth to death.
e. effect of child-rearing practices on basic personality structure.

2. Before the arrival of horses and guns, the Comanche were food foragers in southern Idaho. Their skill as hunters was put to good use as they used these new tools to hunt buffalo on the Great Plains. The term used to refer to existing customs that by chance have potential for a new cultural adaptation is

a. convergent evolution
b. divergent evolution
c. ecosystem
d. parallel evolution
e. preadaptations

3. The Comanche and the Cheyenne were quite different culturally until they moved out onto the Great Plains and made use of the horse to hunt the buffalo and raid settled peoples. They then became more similar in cultural adaptations, a process called

a. preadaptation
b. development of a culture area
c. convergent evolution
d. parallel evolution
e. an ecosystem

4. Native American food foragers established a way of life in New England and southern Quebec that lasted about five thousand years. This is indicative of

a. stagnation.
b. failure to progress.
c. genetic inferiority.
d. lack of innovation.
e. effective cultural adaptation.

5. A culture type is defined by

a. the geographic area in which a people live.
b. the kind of technology that a group has to exploit a particular environment.
c. contacts with other cultures.
d. sharing the same values.
e. sharing the same language.

6. Which of the following could be considered part of a society's "culture core"?

a. the number of hours a people work each day
b. a taboo against eating certain foods
c. the belief that only a chief has strong enough magic to plant apple trees and dispense them to his fellow villagers
d. all of the above
e. none of the above

7. Which of the following research topics might be of interest to an ethnoscientist?

a. How the allele responsible for sickle-cell anemia increases or decreases in certain cultural environments, such as horticultural vs. hunter-gathering.
b. Similarities and differences in the farming patterns of Southwest Asia and Mesoamerica.
c. The ways in which a group classifies and explains the world; for example, the Tsembaga avoid low-lying, marshy areas filled with mosquitoes that carry malaria because they believe that such areas are inhabited by red spirits who punish trespassers.
d. Reconstruction and comparison of archaeological sites in similar geographic regions.
e. all of the above

8. Some anthropologists refer to food foragers as "the original affluent society" because

a. they manage to accumulate a lot of wealth.
b. they occupy the most attractive environments with abundant food supply.
c. they live in marginal areas and are very poor.
d. they earn a good wage for all the hours of work they put in each week.
e. they work only twelve to nineteen hours a week for a comfortable, healthy life.

9. The groups referred to as food foragers must live where there are naturally available food sources; thus they _____.

a. remain in permanent settlements.
b. move about once every ten years.
c. move frequently.
d. adopt farming whenever they can.
e. prefer to live in cities.

10. The number and intensity of interactions among the members of a residential unit is called

a. density of social relations.
b. social interactionism.
c. cultural ecology.
d. carrying capacity.
e. convergent evolution.

11. Which of the following is NOT one of the three elements of human social organization that developed with hunting?

a. sexual division of labor
b. aggressive behavior
c. food sharing
d. the camp site
e. all of the above

12. In a food-foraging society, how do people store food for the future?

a. They keep a surplus in stone cairns.
b. They keep extra plants in large, circular yam houses
c. They hide meat in each individual family residence.
d. They rely on the generosity of others to share food.
e. They keep dried food in a common storage shed.

13. To say that food-foraging societies are egalitarian means that

a. there are no status differences.
b. the only status differences are age and sex.
c. everyone is equal except women.
d. men are usually subordinate to women.
e. children are the center of community life.

14. It is sometimes said that female subservience to men is universal because

a. hunting and warfare are universal.
b. men always do the hunting and go to war.
c. hunting and warfare are associated with power and prestige.
d. all of the above
e. none of the above

15. Someone who uses irrigation, fertilizers, and the plow to produce food on large plots of land is known as a/an

a. horticulturalist.
b. intensive agriculturalist.
c. pastoralist.
d. hunter-gatherer.
e. industrialist.

16. _____ are food producers who specialize in animal husbandry and who consider their way of life to be ideal and central to defining their identities.

a. Food foragers
b. Horticulturalists
c. Intensive agriculturalists
d. Pastoralists
e. Industrialists

17. Aztec society in the sixteenth century

a. was a stratified society based on achievement and education.
b. was an urbanized society in which kinship played no role in determining status.
c. was an industrial city-state.
d. was invincible to Cortes' attack.
e. none of the above

18. Which of the following statements about preindustrial cities is INCORRECT?

a. Preindustrial cities have existed in some parts of the world for thousands of years.
b. Preindustrial cities represent a stage of development in the progression of human culture toward industrial cities.
c. Tenochtitlan, the capital of the Aztec empire, is a good example of a preindustrial city.
d. Preindustrial cities have a diversified economy.
e. Preindustrial cities are highly stratified.

Answers to multiple-choice practice questions

1. a   2. e   3. c   4. e   5. d   6. d   7. c   8. e   9. c   10. a   11. b   12. d
13. b   14. d   15. b   16. d   17. e   18. b

True/False Practice Questions

1. According to the Original Study, the KeKranoti Kayapo had to work hard to get enough produce from their gardens.

2. The Gururumba live in a tropical environment in central Africa.

3. The Bakhtiari are pastoralist nomads who wander throughout the Iran-Iraq border area following their herds.

4. Many Bakhtiari are well-educated, having attended university at home or abroad.

5. The spread of malaria was historically linked to the development of slash-and-burn horticulture.

6. About 3 million people live by food foraging in the world today.

7. People started shifting to food-producing ways of life about ten thousand years ago.

8. The average work week of the Ju/'hoansi is about fifty hours.

9. An anthropologist would probably find it difficult to define what "progress" is.

Answers to true/false practice questions

1. F   2. F   3. F   4. T   5. T   6. F   7. T   8. F   9. T

Practice Matching

1. _____ Tsembaga   a. Highland Peruvian agriculturalists

2. _____ Bakhtiari   b. West Asian pastoralists

3. _____ Comanche   c. Horse people of the Great Plains

4. _____ Gururumba   d. Pig sacrificers of New Guinea

5. _____ Aymara   e. Horticulturalists of New Guinea

Answers to practice matching

1. d   2. b   3. c   4. e   5. a

Practice Essays

1. How does Ju/'hoansi social organization relate to the subsistence pattern of hunting and collecting? How is Ju/'hoansi society likely to change as the foraging way of life is eroded?

2. Think about your neighborhood. Could it be described as a kind of cultural area? What criteria would be important for defining it that way?

Chapter 7
Economic Systems

Synopsis

Chapter 7 discusses the attempt to apply economic theory to non-Western cultures and summarizes the concepts anthropologists have developed to compare the organization of productive resources across cultures. Three major ways of distributing goods and services are described. The relevance of anthropological understanding to international business is also considered.

What You Should Learn from This Chapter

1. Understand how anthropologists study economic systems.
2. Know the patterns of labor in nonindustrial societies:
   • sexual division of labor
   • division of labor by age
   • cooperation
   • craft specialization
   • control of land
   • technology
3. Understand the methods of distribution and exchange in nonindustrial societies:
   • reciprocity
   • redistribution
   • market exchange

Key Terms and Names

technology

leveling mechanism

reciprocity

generalized reciprocity

balanced reciprocity

negative reciprocity

silent trade

redistribution

Kula ring

Big Man

conspicuous consumption

market exchange

money

informal economy

Review Questions

1. Why might it be misleading to apply contemporary economic theories to preindustrial non-Western societies?

2. Explain the importance of yam production among the Trobrianders.

3. Provide examples that refute the notion of a biological division of labor.

4. Compare and contrast the three general patterns of the sexual division of labor.

5. What are the benefits of the division of labor?

6. How is land controlled in most preindustrial societies?

7. Differentiate between the use of tools in foraging, horticultural, and agricultural communities.

8. Distinguish between industrial and nonindustrial societies with regard to craft specialization.

9. How do societies cooperate in the acquisition of food?

10. Provide some examples of leveling mechanisms.

11. Distinguish between market exchange and marketplace.

12. What are three systems of exchange?

13. What purpose does reciprocity serve?

14. Differentiate between general, balanced, and negative reciprocity.

15. How is trade between groups generally conducted?

16. Describe the relationships between the Kota, Toda, Badaga, and Kurumba of India.

17. What functions does the Kula ring serve?

18. Compare "money" among the Aztec and the Tiv.

19. Why is redistribution generally undertaken?

20. Describe the "informal economy" of North America.

21. How is conspicuous consumption used?

22. Discuss the relevance of anthropology to international business.

23. What are the drawbacks of ethnocentric interpretations of other societies' economic systems?

24. Discuss the role that culture plays in defining the "wants and needs" of a people.

Fill-in-the-Blank

1. All societies have rules pertaining to three productive resources: _____, _____, and _____.

2. Division of labor by sex varies from very flexible to very rigid. Among foragers like the _____, either sex may do the work of the other without loss of face.

3. Rigid division of labor by sex typically occurs with two patterns of subsistence: _____ and _____.

4. In most societies the basic unit in which cooperation takes place is the _____.

5. Among horticulturalists, tools that are typically used are the _____, _____, and _____.

6. A _____ works to spread wealth around so that no one accumulates substantially more wealth than anyone else.

7. The economist _____ developed the threefold classification system of reciprocity, redistribution, and market exchange.

8. Types of reciprocity are _____, _____, and _____.

9. The taxation systems of Canada and the United States are examples of _____ systems.

10. In some societies the surplus is used as a display for purposes of prestige. Thorsten Veblen called this _____.

11. Among the Enga of Papua New Guinea, the group that pools its wealth is the _____.

12. The Kota, Toda, Badaga, and Kurumba are interrelated societies in _____.

Exercises

I. When Bronislaw Malinowski studied the Kula ring of the Trobriand Islanders in his classic *Argonauts of the Western Pacific*, he also described other methods of distributing goods in that society as well. Consider each of the following examples of Trobriand exchanges given by Malinowski, and identify whether they can be characterized as forms of reciprocity, redistribution, or market exchange. Then note the elements of each of these forms of exchange in modern North American society as well.

A. *Wasi* : permanent partnerships inland yam-producers inherit with fishermen. When a fisherman brings in a good catch, he takes some fish to his inland partner and gives them as a gift; when the farmer brings in his yam harvest, he takes some to the fisherman as a gift. Neither has any choice about changing partners, neither can bargain for more products, and there is no stated expectation of a return.

B. *Urigubu* : the yam gift that a man gives to his sister's husband every year; it is part of a person's kinship obligations.

C. *Kula* : the exchange between contractual partners of ceremonial/prestige/treasure items.

D. *Pokala* : tribute to a higher-status person, usually a chief.

E. *Sagali* : giveaway feast by a high-status person, usually a chief.

F. *Gim wali* : the moneyless exchange of mundane goods (barter) that occurs after the Kula gift-giving; this exchange occurs between anyone (no contractual partners), and the value seems to be established according to supply and demand and done with a desire to gain the greatest profit.

II. Briefly identify the following cultures, and indicate their locations on the map.

1. Enga   2. Inca

3. Afar   4. Tiv

5. Kota, Toda, Bagada, Kurumba

Multiple-Choice Practice Questions

1. When a man works hard in his horticultural garden in the Trobriand Islands to produce yams, he does this to satisfy which of the following demands?

   a. to have food for his household to eat
   b. to gain prestige by giving yams away to his sisters' husbands
   c. to prove to his wife that he can work as hard as she can
   d. to give the yams to his wife so that she can trade them for goods that they don't produce themselves
   e. to trade for fish

2. The productive resources used by all societies to produce goods and services include

   a. raw materials.
   b. labor.
   c. technology.
   d. all of the above
   e. none of the above

3. American society's traditional sexual division of labor falls into which pattern?

   a. flexible
   b. rigid segregation
   c. segregation with equality
   d. integrated
   e. cooperative

4. Among the Ju/'hoansi,

   a. children are expected to contribute to subsistence from the time they are seven or eight.
   b. elderly people past the age of sixty are expected to contribute hunted or gathered food to the group.
   c. elderly people are a valuable source of knowledge and wisdom about hunting and gathering.
   d. elderly people are taken care of grudgingly because after the age of sixty they contribute nothing to the group.
   e. children are expected to set up their own separate households by the time they are twelve.

5. In many nonindustrial societies,

a. people prefer to have fun rather than to work.
b. cooperative work is usually done with a festive, sociable air.
c. cooperative work is always done in the household.
d. cooperative work groups are organized primarily for profit.
e. solitary work is preferred to cooperative work.

6. Among food foragers such as the Ju/'hoansi,

a. land is defined as a territory with usable resources and flexible boundaries that belongs to a band that has occupied it for a long time.
b. land is thought of as belonging to those who have bought it.
c. land is considered private property, and access to the land can be denied.
d. land has clear-cut boundaries marked by survey posts.
e. land is controlled by a corporation of strangers.

7. In nonindustrial societies, when a tool is complex and difficult to make it is usually considered to be owned by

a. the whole village in which it is used.
b. a single individual.
c. the state.
d. all those who touch it.
e. all relatives.

8. Leveling mechanisms

a. are more common in hunter-gatherer societies than in agricultural communities.
b. result in one family becoming wealthier than others.
c. are found in communities where property must not be allowed to threaten an egalitarian social order.
d. are more common in industrial societies than in agricultural societies.
e. no longer exist.

9. The mode of distribution called reciprocity refers to the exchange of goods and services

a. of unequal value.
b. between persons in hierarchical relationships.
c. for the purpose of maintaining social relationships and gaining prestige.
d. to make a profit.
e. to embarrass the person who gave the least.

10. A Navaho gives ten of his sheep that he knows are infected with disease to a Hopi in exchange for a jeep. This is an example of

a. generalized reciprocity.
b. balanced reciprocity.
c. negative reciprocity.
d. silent trade.
e. redistribution.

11. The Kula ring

a. is a marriage ring made of shells.
b. is found among the Ju'hoansi.
c. is found among the Andaman Islanders.
d. is a circular trade route along which various goods flow.
e. is a form of silent trade.

12. The American system of paying income taxes every April is an example of

a. generalized reciprocity.
b. balanced reciprocity.
c. negative reciprocity.
d. redistribution.
e. market exchange.

13. The display of wealth for social prestige is called

a. a leveling mechanism.
b. conspicuous consumption.
c. redistribution.
d. balanced reciprocity.
e. barter.

14. Market exchange is usually associated with

a. hunting and gathering bands.
b. horticultural tribes.
c. pastoral tribes.
d. a state type of political organization.
e. the household as the unit of production and consumption.

15. A businessperson who wants to build a factory in the Middle East could benefit from the contributions of a cultural anthropologist. In which of the following ways would an anthropologist be likely to help?

a. provide knowledge of the principles of market exchange
b. introduce a new method of paying local workers
c. tell the businessperson how to sit, dress, and talk when making the arrangements with local people
d. screen workers who have diseases
e. provide frequent weather reports

Answers to multiple-choice practice questions

1. b   2. d   3. b   4. c   5. b   6. a   7. b   8. c   9. c   10. c   11. d   12. d
13. b   14. d   15. c

True/False Practice Questions

1. According to Robert Lowie, patterns of reciprocity among the Crow did not involve women.

2. In "silent trade," no words are spoken, but the participants must meet face to face to exchange goods.

3. The Inca empire of Peru featured a highly efficient redistributive system.

4. The economist responsible for the concept of "conspicuous consumption" was Thorsten Veblen.

5. The Enga live in Indonesia.

6. Jomo Keyatta was an anthropologist who became "the father" of modern Kenya.

Answers to true/false practice questions

1. F   2. F   3. T   4. T   5. F   6. T

Practice Essays

1. Compare and contrast the different ideas about the nature and control of land that exist among food foragers, horticulturalists, pastoralists, intensive agriculturalists, and industrialists.

2. Compare and contrast the different ideas about tools and tool ownership in foraging, horticultural, and intensive agricultural societies.

3. Describe the ecological context of the "Big Man" system of the Enga.

Chapter 8
Sex and Marriage

Synopsis

Chapter 8 defines marriage as a system for regulating sexual access and explores the variations on the theme of marriage throughout the world. The interactions of marriage, social structure, and environment are considered.

What You Should Learn from This Chapter

1. Understand what marriage is in nonethnocentric terms.
2. Know the controls societies place on sexual relations and theories as to why these controls are necessary.
3. Understand the many forms of marriage and how they correlate with other aspects of society:
   • monogamy
   • polygyny
   • polyandry
   • two forms of cousin marriage
4. Understand the role of consanguineal and affinal ties in society.
5. Know the kinds of gift exchanges that often accompany marriage.

Key Terms and Names

marriage

Claude Levi-Strauss

affinal kin

conjugal bond

consanguineal kin

incest taboo

endogamy

exogamy

monogamy

family

consanguine family

nuclear family

polygyny

polyandry

group marriage

levirate

sororate

serial monogamy

patrilateral parallel-cousin marriage

matrilateral cross-cousin marriage

bride price

bride service

dowry

Review Questions

1. Why are human females able to engage in sexual activity regardless of their ovulation cycles?

2. Why does sexual activity require social control?

3. Describe the sex life of the Trobrianders.

4. Describe the marriage system of the Nayar.

5. What is the incest taboo?

6. Why do people living in close proximity to one another exhibit reduced sexual activity?

7. What are the Oedipus and Electra complexes?

8. How have geneticists attempted to explain the incest taboo?

9. Distinguish between endogamy and exogamy.

10. What were the initial reasons for exogamy, according to Tylor, Levi-Strauss, and Cohen?

11. Distinguish between marriage and mating.

12. To what extent can North American society be characterized as monogamous?

13. Provide a nonethnocentric definition of marriage.

14. Distinguish between consanguineal and conjugal families.

15. Distinguish between polygynous and polyandrous families.

16. What form of marriage does the majority of the world's societies exhibit?

17. Characterize the typical polygynous society.

18. What is the attitude of Kapauku women towards their husbands' other wives?

19. Describe the social and economic context of polyandry.

20. Discuss the contexts in which sororate, levirate, and serial monogamy are likely to occur.

21. What benefits do arranged marriages have?

22. Describe the marriage system of Sidi Embarek, Morocco.

23. Distinguish between patrilateral parallel-cousin and matrilateral cross-cousin marriage.

24. How is marriage exchange conducted among the Trobrianders?

25. Distinguish between bride price, dowry, and bride service.

26. What is the function of female-female marriage among the Nandi?

27. What role can anthropologists play in the study of AIDS?

Fill-in-the-Blank

1. Marriage is a cultural transaction that regulates men and women's rights of _____ access to one another and defines the context in which women are eligible to bear children.

2. The female ability to engage is sexual relations at any time is related to the development of _____ locomotion among the hominines.

3. Only about _____ percent of the world's societies prohibit all sexual involvement outside of marriage.

4. The bond between two individuals joined by marriage is called a(n) _____ bond.

5. Households composed only of "blood" relatives are said to contain _____ kin.

6. The _____ taboo prohibits sexual relations between specified individuals.

7. _____ is a rule mandating that one marry outside of a particular group, while _____ mandates marriage within the group.

8. In the United States, _____ is the only legally recognized form of marriage, but some Americans do engage in other forms.

9. A _____ family contains a husband and his multiple wives, while a _____ family contains a wife and her multiple husbands.

10. Among the Turkana of northern Kenya, _____ is the perferred form of marriage.

11. When the wives in a polygynous marriage are sisters, this is called _____ polygyny.

12. _____ marriage refers to a marriage in which several men and women have sexual access to one another.

13. In a _____, a widow marries the brother of her deceased husband; in a _____, a widower marries the sister of his deceased wife.

14. Marrying a sequence of partners throughout one's life is called _____.

15. In a patrilateral parallel-cousin marriage, a boy marries his father's _____ daughter.

16. _____ is a gift exhange occuring at marriage in which money or goods are transferred from the groom's side to the bride's.

17. In a _____ system, the bride's family provides money or goods at the time of marriage.

18. The Nandi of western Kenya practice a form of marriage in which a woman marries _____.

19. Divorce rates in Western society are considered high by many people but are low compared to divorce rates among _____ societies.

20. _____ is a French anthropologist who launched a school of thought called structuralism.

21. Medical anthropologists can contribute significantly to the study of _____ through investigating the social and sexual contexts of disease transmission in various societies.

Exercises

I. Draw your family tree in the space below. Make it as extensive as you can without consulting any of your relatives. What accounts for the relatively truncated kindreds of most North Americans?

II. Briefly identify and locate the following cultures on the map.

1. Nayar   2. Nandi

3. Morocco   4. Tibet

Multiple-Choice Practice Questions

1. _____ is a transaction in which a woman and man establish a continuing claim to the right of sexual access to one another, and in which the woman involved becomes eligible to bear children.

a. Family
b. Marriage
c. Incest
d. Affinity
e. Sex

2. One explanation for the tendency of human females to be sexually receptive on a continuing basis is that

a. it is an accidental byproduct of the high hormone requirements for persistent bipedal locomotion.
b. it increases competitiveness among the males of a group.
c. it encourages endogamy.
d. it discourages incest.
e. it leads to greater competitiveness among women.

3. Marriage resolves the problem of how to bring sexual activity under _____ control.

a. biological
b. male
c. cultural
d. female
e. mother-in-law

4. A household composed of married people contains _____ kin.

a. affinal
b. consanguineal
c. endogamous
d. nuclear
e. instinctive

5. According to the _____ theory of incest taboo, children feel so guilty about their sexual feelings for a parent that they repress them, and this is expressed culturally in the incest taboo.

a. genetic
b. instinctive
c. psychological
d. anthropological
e. sociological

6. Although all societies have some kind of incest taboo, the relationship that is considered incestuous may vary. Concepts of incest seem to be related to a group's definitions of endogamy and exogamy, thus suggesting that incest taboos may help to promote

a. alliances between groups.
b. inbreeding.
c. brother-sister marriages.
d. parallel-cousin marriages.
e. cross-cousin marriages.

7. Marriage within a particular group of individuals is called

a. incest.
b. exogamy.
c. monogamy.
d. endogamy.
e. polygamy.

8. The French anthropologist Claude Levi-Strauss says that the incest taboo is universal because humans

a. are instinctively opposed to inbreeding.
b. repress their sexual desire for the parent of the opposite sex.
c. have learned to establish alliances with strangers and thereby share and develop culture.
d. prefer to marry their brothers and sisters.
e. don't like sex.

9. A residential kin group composed of a woman, her dependent children, and at least one adult male joined through marriage or blood relationship is a/an

a. family.
b. conjugal bond.
c. endogamous group.
d. nuclear family.
e. serial marriage.

10. Families can be consanguineal or conjugal. The conjugal family has many forms. One type of conjugal family is the _____, consisting of the husband, wife, and dependent children.

a. polygynous family
b. polygamous family
c. polyandrous family
d. nuclear family
e. extended family

11. The most common form of marriage is

a. polygyny.
b. monogamy.
c. polyandry.
d. polygamy.
e. the levirate.

12. Polygyny

a. means marriage to more than one man.
b. is the most common form of marriage.
c. is possible only when a man is fairly wealthy.
d. is less common than polyandry.
e. is an example of group marriage.

13. An example of group marriage would be

a. a pastoral nomad's wife among the Turkana who actively searches for another woman to share her husband and her work with the livestock.
b. the Moonies having a large wedding ceremony at which five hundred couples, each one assigned to another, are married at the same time.
c. a prosperous member of the Kapauku in western New Guinea who is able to afford a bride price for four wives.
d. a hippy commune in the Haight-Ashbury district in which it is accepted that all adult members of the commune have sexual access to each other.
e. a Nayar household in which a woman takes several lovers.

14. The levirate and the sororate

a. are secret societies, like sororities and fraternities.
b. function to maintain the relationship between the family of the bride and the family of the groom.
c. do not work if the surviving spouse was an only child.
d. are types of cattle in pastoralist societies.
e. exist only in advanced industrial societies.

15. Serial monogamy tends to occur in societies where

a. a woman with children receives a great deal of help from her mother and brothers.
b. women do not have many children.
c. a woman with dependent children, isolated from her parents, marries a series of partners to get the assistance of another adult.
d. women are very wealthy.
e. divorce is forbidden.

16. The main function of a bride price is

a. for a man to show off to his wife how rich he is.
b. for a man to buy a slave.
c. for the wife's people to gain prestige in the village.
d. to strengthen the stability of the marriage.
e. for the wife's people to buy a husband for their daughter.

17. When a a man marries his father's brother's daughter in ancient Greece or traditional China,

a. he is committing incest.
b. he is practicing matrilateral cross-cousin marriage.
c. he is practicing patrilateral cross-cousin marriage.
d. he is keeping property within the single male line of descent.
e. *c* and *d*

18. In which of the following situations would you expect to find the custom of bride price?

a. A bride and groom leave the community after marriage and set up their own household in a distant city.
b. A bride and groom go to live with the bride's people.
c. A bride and groom go to live with the groom's people.
d. A bride and groom go to live with the bride's mother's brother.
e. none of the above

19. When the economy is based on _____ and where the man does most of the productive work, the bride's people may give a dowry that protects the woman against desertion and is a statement of her economic status.

a. food foraging
b. pastoralism
c. intensive agriculture
d. horticulture
e. industrialism

20. The woman/woman marriage custom found in sub-Saharan Africa

a. enables a woman without sons to inherit a share of her husband's property.
b. confers legitimacy on the children of a woman who had been unable to find a husband.
c. enables the woman who adopts a male identity to raise her status.
d. enables the woman who is the wife of the female husband to raise her status and live a more secure life.
e. all of the above

21. Which of the following constitutes a culturally valid reason for divorce among different human groups?

a. sterility or impotence
b. cruelty
c. being a poor provider
d. being a lazy housekeeper
e. all of the above

Answers to multiple-choice practice questions

1. b   2. a   3. c   4. a   5. c   6. a   7. d   8. c   9. a   10. d   11. b   12. c
13. d   14. b   15. c   16. d   17. e   18. c   19. c   20. e   21. e

True/False Practice Questions

1. Trobriand children begin sexual experimentation at a young age.

2. About half of the world's societies prohibit sexual involvement outside of marriage.

3. Haviland believes that evidence on intrafamily homicides support Freud's theories of the Oedipus and Electra complexes.

4. Brother-sister marriages were common among farmers in Roman Egypt.

5. Primate evidence shows that it is likely that humans started out as a monogamous species.

Answers to true/false practice questions

1. T   2. F   3. F   4. T   5. F

Practice Matching

Match the culture with its characteristic.

1. _____ Nandi

2. _____ Moroccans

3. _____ Nayar

4. _____ Tibetans

5. _____ North Americans

a. A culture emphasizing love and choice as a basis for marriage

b. South Indian people who give the mother's brothers key responsibility in child rearing

c. Patrilineal North African people who practice arranged marriage

d. East African pastoralists who practice woman/woman marriage

e. Polyandrous society of central Asia

Answers to practice matching

1. d   2. c   3. b   4. e   5. a

Practice Essays

1. Describe how the "romantic love" complex impacts North American marriage patterns, and explore how it is tied into the broader social structure of the society.

2. What factors affect the stability of marriages and the choice of mates?

Chapter 9
Family and Household

Synopsis

Chapter 9 focuses on the differences between families and households, noting that the Western assumption that all households are built around conjugal relationships is ethnocentric. The major residence patterns are defined, and the various problems engendered by different kinds of living arrangements are explored.

What You Should Learn from This Chapter

1. Understand the functions of the family in human society and the difference between family and household.
2. Know the various forms of family organization and the difficulties associated with each:
   • polygynous
   • extended
   • nuclear
   • female-headed
3. Know the basic kinds of residence rules that are found in diverse societies:
   • patrilocal
   • matrilocal
   • ambilocal
   • neolocal
   • avunculocal

Key Terms

household

conjugal family

extended family

patrilocal residence

matrilocal residence

ambilocal residence

neolocal residence

avunculocal residence

Review Questions

1. How does Haviland define "family?"

2. How did historical and social circumstances shape the character of the Western family?

3. Describe the nurturing requirement of primates.

4. Describe the various ways in which households can be structured.

5. How is the modern American family related to the rise of industrial capitalism?

6. Describe the nuclear family.

7. What relations might be a part of the extended family?

8. What societal factors might contribute to the existence of extended families?

9. Distinguish the five common patterns of residence.

10. How does ecology impact residence pattern?

11. What residence pattern was traditionally followed by people along the Maine coast and why?

12. What residence pattern was traditionally followed by the Hopi and what was its impact on family life?

13. What problems may accompany polygynous families and how are they dealt with?

14. What problems may accompany extended families and how are they dealt with?

15. What problems may accompany nuclear families and how are they dealt with?

16. What problems may accompany female-headed families and how are they dealt with?

17. How was Dr. Margaret Boone able to impact policies relating to infant mortality in Washington, D.C.?

18. How does the status of women relate to various kinds of family and residence patterns?

Fill-in-the-Blank

1. The independent nuclear family emerged in Europe in the fourth century A.D. in respose to regulations put forward by _____.

2. The "ephemeral modern family" that developed in conjunction with industrial capitalism was studied by _____.

3. A family based on a marital tie is called a _____ family, while a family based on blood ties is called a _____ family.

4. A _____ is a residential group composed of a woman, her dependent children, and at least one male joined through marriage or a blood relationship.

5. Among the Mundurucu, after age thirteen boys go to live in _____.

6. Two examples of the rare consanguineal family are the _____ and the _____.

7. Two examples of societies based on independent nuclear families are the _____ and the _____.

8. In a _____ form of residence, husbands go to live with their wife's parents after marriage.

9. In a _____ form of residence, wives go to live with their husband's parents after marriage.

10. The Hopi practice _____ residence while the Chinese practice _____ residence.

11. Among the Trobrianders, a newly married couple goes to live with the groom's mother's brother. This is called _____ residence.

12. The Mbuti practice _____ residence.

13. Dr. Margaret Boone studied the problem of _____ in Washington, D.C.

Exercises

I. Anthropologists have developed a method of expressing kin relationships symbolically. In this
    form of notation, males are represented by triangles and females by circles. A bond of
    marriage is represented by an equal sign (two parallel lines) while a consanguineal bond is
    represented by a single line. For example, the following diagram shows a conventional nuclear
    family of a husband, wife, and two children:

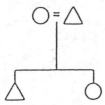

There are further specifications possible in the standard genealogical notation. If an individual
is deceased, he or she is represented by a diagonal line drawn through the triangle or circle.
Here is a diagram of a widow with her three sons and one daughter. In the society in which
this hypothetical family lives, goods are inherited through the female line, from mother to
daughter. This is indicated on the diagram by coloring in the triangles and circles in the line of
inheritence (the lineage).

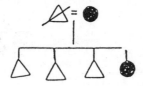

Sometimes other kinds of modifications can be added to a genealogical chart as well. For
example, a residence group might be indicated by drawing a line around the individuals
included in the household. For example, the following shows an extended family household
based on ties between brothers.

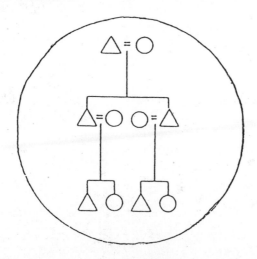

Now redraw your family tree from Chapter 8 using standard genealogical notation. (Don't worry about inheritance or residence here; just diagram the basic affinal and consanguineal ties.)

II. On the three charts below, illustrate a *patrilocal* residence group, a *matrilocal* residence group, and an *avunculocal* residence group by drawing a line around the included individuals.

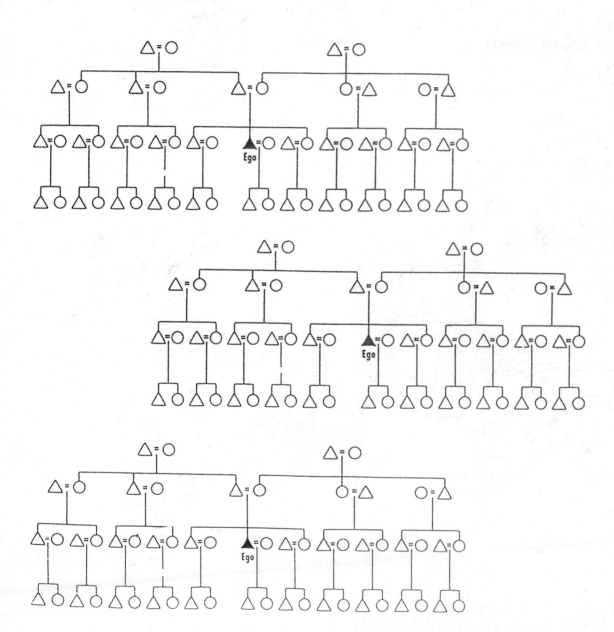

126

III. Briefly identify and locate the following cultures:

1. Mundurucu   2. Tory Islanders

3. Coastal Mainers   4. Inuit

5. Hopi

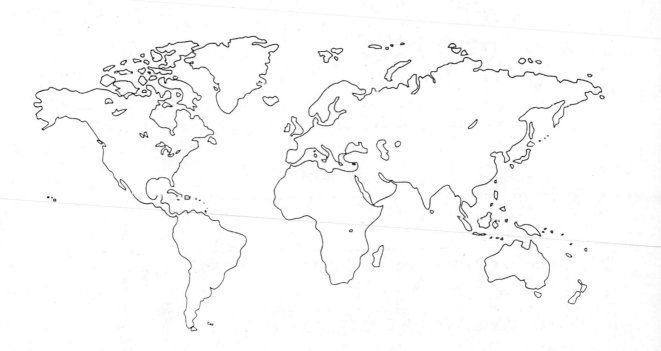

Multiple-Choice Practice Questions

1. The independent nuclear family in Europe

a. emerged recently as the result of regulations passed by the Roman Catholic Church in the fourth century A.D.
b. is a universal family form that is natural to primates.
c. is found only in Europe and places to which Europeans have emigrated.
d. is found only in non-Western societies.
e. was the only form of family considered legitimate in the Old Testament of the Bible.

2. The effect of industrialization on nuclear families was

a. an increased dependence on extended kin, who could provide aid during difficult times.
b. greater isolation because of the mobility required of an industrial labor force.
c. greater conflict among members of the nuclear family over scarce jobs.
d. the tendency to develop polygyny.
e. the tendency to develop the levirate.

3. Which of the following statements is CORRECT?

a. The period of infant dependency in humans is the same as that in other primates.
b. The family is the only unit in which children can be reared in a nurturant manner.
c. Only among humans are males larger and stronger than females.
d. Human infants can survive only with the care provided by the biological mother.
e. none of the above is correct.

4. A household is

a. a residential group composed of a woman, her dependent children, and at least one male joined through marriage or consanguineal relationship.
b. a nonresidential group composed of people who share common interests.
c. a residential unit within which economic production, consumption, inheritance, child rearing and shelter are organized and carried out.
d. a temporary association of strangers.
e. a research center.

5. A residential kin group composed of related women, their brothers, and the women's offspring is

a. a conjugal family
b. an extended family
c. a consanguineal family
d. a nuclear family
e. a patrilocal family

6. What do traditional Inuit society and contemporary North American society have in common that explains the similarity in their family structure?

a. Both developed in arctic environments.
b. Both rely on the technology of hunting.
c. In both, people have very few possessions so there is little jealousy.
d. Both care for their elderly.
e. Both are highly mobile.

7. The _____ is composed of people related to each other by ties of blood who bring their spouses to live in the family.

a. extended family
b. polygamous family
c. consanguine family
d. nuclear family
e. communal family

8. Residence patterns refer to

a. how a group makes its living in a particular environment.
b. the structure of a family under certain ecological conditions.
c. where a couple chooses to live after they are married.
d. the problems that different families have.
e. whether the husband and wife sleep in the same room or in different rooms after they are married.

9. Societies that rely on animal husbandry or intensive agriculture, in which polygyny is customary and where warfare is prominent enough to make male cooperation important, are most likely to practice _____ residence.

a. matrilocal
b. avunculocal
c. ambilocal
d. patrilocal
e. neolocal

10. Ambilocal residence is found in societies

a. that stress the cooperation of women.
b. where warfare is common and men wield authority.
c. where economic activity occurs outside the family, and families have to move frequently in search of jobs.
d. where males control property but descent and inheritance are reckoned through women.
e. where the nuclear family is not sufficient to handle the economic activities required for the family's survival, but resources are limited.

11. Neolocal residence is common in industrial societies like our own because

a. newlyweds do not usually get along with their in-laws.
b. industries require workers to be able to move to wherever there are jobs.
c. most families set up their own businesses, and they do not require the labor of other family members outside the nuclear family.
d. brothers need to stay together for purposes of conducting warfare.
e. women continue to live with their brothers after marriage.

12. Which of the following statements about residence patterns in the Trobriand Islands is INCORRECT?

a. All couples live with the husband's mother's brother.
b. Men who are in line to take over control of their descent group's assets will take their wives to live with their mother's brother.
c. Most couples live patrilocally.
d. Men who live with their fathers gain access to land controlled by their fathers' descent groups.
e. Men who live with their fathers also have access to land controlled through female descent.

13. A man who marries several sisters is practicing

a. avunculocal residence.
b. sororal polygyny.
c. fraternal polyandry.
d. infidelity.
e. matrilocal residence.

14. Extended families usually work more effectively if authority is in the hands of one person, such as the eldest son. Which of the following methods of reducing conflict between this eldest son and his younger brothers are likely to be found in extended families?

a. moving out of the household
b. dependence training
c. independence training
d. increasing the number of wives for the younger sons
e. murder of the eldest son

15. Extended families have which of the following problems?

a. loneliness caused by isolation from kin
b. Children are raised to be independent, which competes with group harmony.
c. The eldest son is in competition with his younger brothers for the position of authority in the household.
d. all of the above
e. none of the above

16. What are some of the problems associated with the nuclear family?

a. Husbands and wives tend to be isolated from their kin.
b. There are no clear-cut lines of authority and rules for making decisions.
c. The elderly cannot depend on their children for aid when they are too old to take care of themselves.
d. all of the above.
e. none of the above.

17. The increase in number of single-parent households headed by women is likely to be associated with

a. increased child support being paid by fathers.
b. increased participation of extended kin in caring for the children.
c. increased number of women below the poverty line.
d. decreased number of welfare programs.
e. decreased number of women below the poverty line in third-world countries.

Answers to multiple-choice practice questions

1. e   2. b   3. e   4. c   5. c   6. e   7. a   8. c   9. d   10. d   11. b   12. c
13. b   14. b   15. c   16. d   17. c

True/False Practice Questions

1. A woman who marries several brothers is practicing sororal polygyny.

2. Neolocal residence is common when the nuclear family must be able to move independently.

3. Among the Mundurucu, the men's houses and the women's houses constitute separate families.

4. Among the Hopi, daughters brought their husbands to live near their mother's house.

5. In an avunculocal residence pattern, the newly married couple goes to live with the bride's father's sister.

Answers to true/false practice questions

1. F   2. T   3. F   4. T   5. F

Practice Matching

Match the culture with its characteristic.

1. _____ Inuit

2. _____ Coastal Mainers

3. _____ Mundurucu

4. _____ Tory Islanders

5. _____ Hopi

a. Irish society centered on consanguineal families

b. Amazon people with "men's houses"

c. Americans maintaining an extended family tradition

d. Southwestern Native Americans with female-headed families

e. Arctic people who live in nuclear families

Answers to practice matching

1. e   2. c   3. b   4. a   5. d

Practice Essay

Senator Daniel Patrick Moynihan was the author of a classic study on the problems of urban black people in the United States. Known as "the Moynihan report," this document blamed irresponsible males and the resultant female-headed families for many of the ills that plague the African-American community. How might an anthropologist respond to this claim?

(In fact, an anthropologist did respond to it. Her name is Carol Stack and her book *All Our Kin* was a significant landmark in our understanding of African-American culture. You might like to have a look at both the Moynihan report and *All Our Kin* to see how anthropological insights can contribute to more appropriate government policies.)

Chapter 10
Kinship and Descent

Synopsis

Chapter 10 presents some key concepts relating to the anthropological study of kinship and descent. The relationship of kinship patterns to other elements of social organization is explored.

What You Should Learn from This Chapter

1. Know the difference between kindreds and lineal descent groups.
2. Understand the various types of descent systems:
   • patrilineal
   • matrilineal
   • double descent
   • ambilineal
3. Understand the organization and function of descent groups:
   • lineage
   • clan
   • phratry
   • moiety
4. Recognize the major systems of kinship terminology:
   • Eskimo
   • Hawaiian
   • Iroquois
   • Crow
   • Omaha
   • Descriptive

Key Terms and Names

descent group

Lewis Henry Morgan

unilineal descent

matrilineal descent

patrilineal descent

double descent

ambilineal descent

lineage

fission

clan

totemism

phratry

moiety

kindred

Eskimo system

Hawaiian system

Iroquois system

Crow system

Omaha system

Sudanese or Descriptive system

Review Questions

1. Why do societies form descent groups?

2. How is membership in a descent group restricted?

3. Distinguish between patrilineal and matrilineal descent groups.

4. What function does double descent serve in Yakö society?

5. Explain the functions of ambilineal descent in contemporary North America. Provide an example.

6. What functions do descent groups serve?

7. How is a lineage determined?

8. What are the social implications of lineage exogamy?

9. Contrast a clan and a lineage.

10. What did anthropologist Margery Wolf find out about the situation of women in Taiwan?

11. What purpose do totems serve a clan?

12. Distinguish between a phratry and a moiety.

13. How do bilateral systems differ from unilateral systems?

14. What are the functions and limitations of ego-centered groups?

15. Why do descent groups emerge?

16. What functions do kinship terminologies serve?

17. What are the six major systems of kinship?

18. What is the emphasis in the Eskimo system of descent?

19. What is the simplest descent system? Why?

20. With which type of descent group is Iroquois terminology commonly correlated?

21. How can anthropologists assist Native Americans in their struggles for federal recognition?

Exercises

I. On the two charts provided below, color in a *matrilineal descent group* and a *patrilineal descent group*.

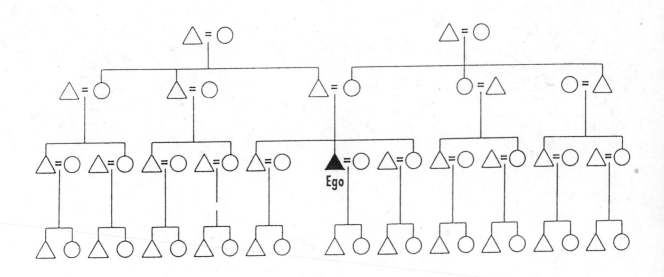

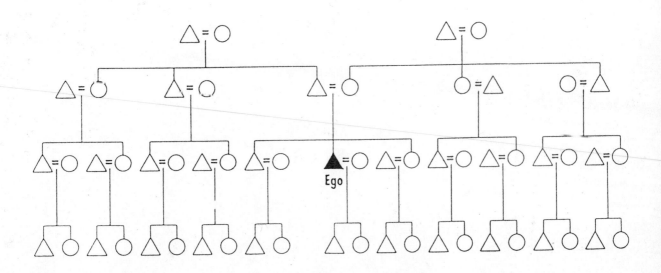

II. What kind of terminological system is shown here?

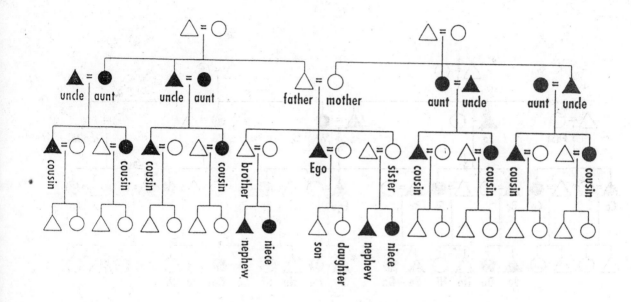

III. What kind of terminological system is shown here?

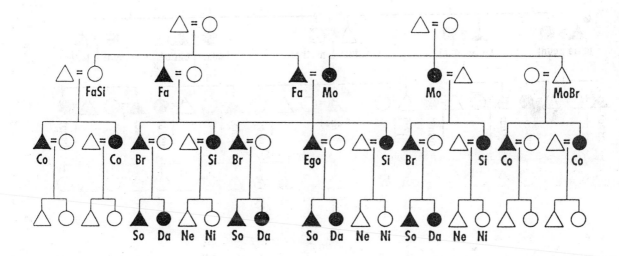

IV. What kind of terminological system is shown here?

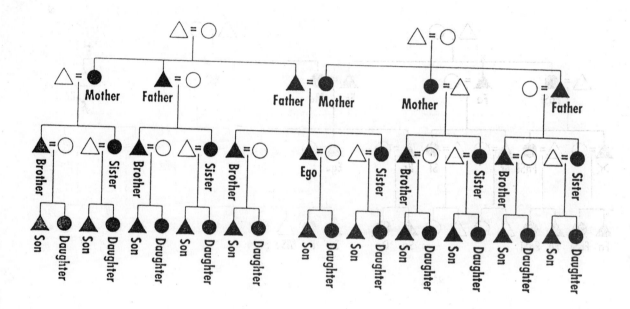

V. In the system below, what should Ego call the individual marked "X"?

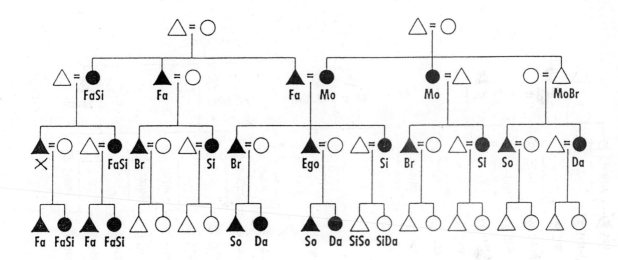

VI. On the chart below, illustrate a descriptive type terminological system.

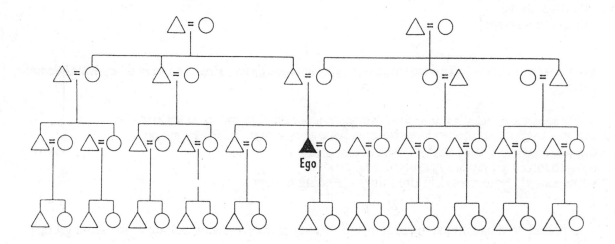

Multiple-Choice Practice Questions

1. Descent groups

a. are composed of those who claim to be lineally descended from a particular ancestor.
b. are common in human societies.
c. trace their connections back to a common ancestor through a chain of parent-child links, and thus appear to stem from the parent-child bond.
d. all of the above
e. none of the above

2. By tracing membership either through males or through females, members of unilineal descent groups

a. know exactly to which group they belong and where their primary loyalties lie.
b. are confused about their relationship to persons not included in the group.
c. act like females if they are in a matrilineal group.
d. act like males if they are in a patrilineal group.
e. know exactly how many children they are going to have.

3. You belong to a patrilineal descent group. Which of the following belong to the same group?

a. your mother
b. your father's sister
c. your mother's sister
d. your mother's father
e. your father's sister's children

4. The primary way in which a woman in traditional China could exert any influence was

a. through her close tie with her husband.
b. by appealing to her mother-in-law who will intercede with her husband on her behalf.
c. by threatening to return to her own people.
d. through the influence of her brothers.
e. through the village women's gossip which can cause a loss of face for her husband and father-in-law.

5. A boy is born into a society that practices matrilineal descent. The person who exercises authority over him is

a. his sister.
b. his father.
c. his mother.
d. his mother's brother.
e. his father's sister.

6. Among the Yako of Nigeria, an individual might inherit grazing lands from his father's patrilineal group, and livestock and ritual knowledge from his mother's matrilineal group. This is an example of _____ descent.

a. ambilineal
b. bilocal
c. patrilateral
d. indivisible
e. double

7. A cousins club

a. is an ambilineal descent group to which younger-generation descendants of east European Jewish immigrants belong.
b. is a double descent group to which only cross cousins belong.
c. is a patrilineal descent group composed of the children of Norman Cousins.
d. is a cognatic descent group composed of women only.
e. is a unlineal descent group for first and second cousins.

8. Descent groups

a. are economic units providing mutual aid.
b. provide social security for elderly members.
c. often promote solidarity by encouraging worship of the group's ancestors.
d. play a role in deciding appropriate marriage partners.
e. all of the above

9. A lineage is a corporate descent group

a. composed of consanguineal kin.
b. the members of which claim descent from a common ancestor.
c. the members of which know the exact genealogical linkages by which they are related to the common ancestor.
d. all of the above
e. none of the above

10. A totem

a. is a word that comes from the Ojibwa American Indian word that means "he is a relative of mine."
b. is a symbol of animals, plants, natural forces, and objects.
c. is usually associated with a clan's concept of its mythical origins.
d. may be found in our own society in the names we give to baseball and football teams.
e. all of the above

11. A phratry is a unilineal descent group composed of two or more _____ that believe they are related to each other.

a. moieties
b. totems
c. kindred
d. lineages
e. clans

12. Members of a moiety

a. belong to one of two major descent groups in a society.
b. are those who are divorced (they lack their "better half").
c. are usually able to trace their exact genealogical links to their common ancestor.
d. feel a much stronger feeling of kinship than is felt by members of a lineage or clan.
e. belong to a group that is smaller than a lineage.

13. A person in a system of bilateral descent

a. traces descent through the father for some purposes, and through the mother for other purposes.
b. traces descent through female lines.
c. traces descent through male lines.
d. uses totems to symbolically represent the group.
e. traces descent through both parents simultaneously and recognizes multiple ancestors.

14. Descent groups are frequently found to be important organizing devices in

a. food-foraging societies.
b. horticultural societies.
c. pastoral societies.
d. intensive agricultural societies.
e. all of the above except a

15. _____ develop out of extended families when families split up and move to nearby regions, and the core members of these families recognize their descent from a common ancestor and continue to organize activities based on this idea.

a. Phratries
b. Kindred groups
c. Lineages
d. Moieties
e. Cognatic groups

16. If two people are given the same kinship term, this means that

a. they have the same genes.
b. no one can tell the difference between them.
c. they occupy a similar status.
d. they are identical twins.
e. they are members of an adopted family.

17. In _____ kinship terminology, ego's "brother" and "sister" are distinguished from "cousins"; both ego's father's brother and mother's brother are given the same kinship term, "uncle."

a. Eskimo
b. Hawaiian
c. Crow
d. Omaha
e. Iroquois

18. In the _____ system of kinship terminology, ego's father, father's brother, and mother's brother are all referred to by the same term, and ego's mother, mother's sister, and father's sister are all referred to by the same term; the term "brother" includes ego's brothers as well as male cousins.

a. Iroquois
b. Crow
c. Omaha
d. Hawaiian
e. Eskimo

19. In _____ kinship terminology, the term "brother" is given to ego's brother, father's brother's son, and mother's sister's son; a different term is used for the sons of father's sister and mother's brother. "Mother" refers to ego's mother and mother's sister; "father" refers to ego's father and father's brother. Separate terms are used for ego's mother's brother and father's sister.

a. Eskimo
b. Hawaiian
c. Iroquois
d. cognatic
e. kindred

20. The Crow kinship terminology system

a. is associated with matrilineal descent.
b. merges paternal cross-cousins with the parent's generation.
c. merges maternal cross-cousins with the generation of ego's children.
d. all of the above
e. none of the above

21. The Omaha kinship terminology system

a. is associated with patrilineal descent.
b. merges maternal cross-cousins with the parental generation.
c. merges paternal cross-cousins with the generation of ego's children.
d. identifies maternal cross-cousins with the lineage of ego's mother (the lineage that supplies women to ego's patrilineage).
e. all of the above

22. The descriptive system of kinship terminology

a. gives the same kinship term for ego's mother's brother and father's brother.
b. is the most common form of kinship terminology.
c. gives a separate term for each kind of cousin.
d. is the least precise of all the kinship systems.
e. indicates that all of ego's siblings have the same social status.

Answers to multiple-choice practice questions

1. d   2. a   3. b   4. e   5. d   6. e   7. a   8. e   9. d   10. e   11. e   12. a
13. e   14. e   15. c   16. c   17. a   18. d   19. c   20. d   21. e   22. c

True/False Practice Questions

1. Cross-cousins are ideal marriage partners in an arrangement whereby lineages engage in reciprocal marriage exchanges to establish alliances.

2. Omaha kinship terminology is the matrilineal equivalent of the Crow system.

3. The system with the greatest number of kin terms is the Sudanese or Descriptive system.

4. The kindred is a kin group that is organized laterally rather than lineally.

5. The boundaries of a kindred are permanent and definite.

Answers to true/false practice questions

1. T   2. F   3. T   4. T   5. F

Practice Essays

1. Compare and contrast the social organization of the Hopi and the Chinese.

2. Many North American feminists are interested in the concept of matriarchy, somtimes confusing it with or linking it to the matrilineal descent system. Does matrilineality imply matriarchy? Use concrete examples to explore this.

Chapter 11
Grouping by Sex, Age, Common Interest, and Class

Synopsis

Chapter 11 examines major kinds of nonkin organizations. Groups defined by gender, age and common interest are described. Finally, stratified forms of social organization such as those involving class or caste are presented.

What You Should Learn from This Chapter

1. Understand the functions of nonkin groupings:
   • sex
   • age
   • common interest
2. Know how societies are stratified and the reasons for social divisions.
3. Understand the differences between class and caste-type stratification.

Key Terms

age grade

age set

cousins clubs

common-interest association

stratified society

egalitarian society

social class

caste

apartheid

verbal evaluation

symbolic indicators

mobility

open-class societies

Review Questions

1. Describe the separate but equal organization of the Iroquois.

2. In what ways is age grouping evidenced in North America?

3. How does one become a member of an age grade?

4. Distinguish between an age group and an age set.

5. Describe the Tiriki age-set system.

6. How and why are common-interest associations formed?

7. Historically, why have women's groups been less common than men's?

8. What functions do women's associations serve?

9. What purposes do urban-oriented associations serve?

10. Describe the interstrata relationship in a stratified society.

11. Contrast an egalitarian society with a stratified society.

12. In what ways might a society be stratified?

13. Briefly describe India's caste system.

14. Compare India's caste system to the South African system of apartheid.

15. How might a stratified society beget an outcast group?

16. What are three aspects of a social-class structure?

17. Distinguish between the three ways social classes are manifest in society.

18. What is social-impact assessment?

19. What role does religion play in India's caste system?

20. How and why did the Maya develop a stratified society?

Fill-in-the-Blank

1. An age _____ is a category based on age, a stage through which people pass (such as "teenager").

2. An age _____ is a group of people who move through life stages together (such as "baby boomers").

3. Among the _____ of South America, men and women work, eat, and sleep separately.

4. Common-interest associations used to be called _____ associations.

5. The text suggests that caste is present not only in India but also in _____ and _____.

6. A _____ society is one in which members do not share equally in prestige and basic resources.

7. _____ is a special form of social class in which membership is determined by birth and remains fixed for life.

8. In a class society, people are theoretically able to change their class positions through social _____.

Exercise

Briefly identify and locate the following cultures.

1. Iroquois   2. South African

3. Tiriki   4. Maya

Multiple-Choice Practice Questions

1. High rates of rape appear to be associated with societies in which the roles of males and females are highly segregated, and in which there are efforts by males to be dominant over women. If this is true, we would expect the highest rate of rape to occur among the

    a. Ju/'hoansi.
    b. Mundurucu.
    c. Iroquois.
    d. Mbuti.
    e. Hopi.

2. Ambilineal descent groups were a response among Jewish immigrants to urban life in North America. These groups did not recruit on the basis of age. By the late 1930s, their descendants had become so assimilated that they formed new descent groups, called _____, which excluded their parents and grandparents from membership as well as their own children until they reached legal majority or married.

    a. family circles
    b. cousins clubs
    c. age grades
    d. age sets
    e. common-interest associations

3. In literate societies that rely on the written word for accumulated wisdom, elders are often

    a. treated with great respect because of their wisdom.
    b. considered to be as valuable as their weight in gold.
    c. treated like "living libraries" that contain much needed knowledge.
    d. not considered sources of information; they tend to be ignored.
    e. killed when they turn sixty-five years old.

4. The following _____ are passed through by members of North American culture: toddler, teenager, senior citizen.

    a. age grades
    b. age sets
    c. social classes
    d. castes
    e. open classes

5. Which of the following statements about common-interest associations is INCORRECT?

a. They were originally referred to in the anthropological literature as voluntary associations.
b. Common-interest associations are more common in hunter-gatherer societies than in urban -industrial societies.
c. Common-interest associations are intimately associated with world urbanization and increasing social complexity.
d. Common-interest associations are found in many traditional societies.
e. Sometimes one can join a common-interest association voluntarily, and sometimes membership is required by law.

6. The text suggests that women's participation in common-interest associations in traditional societies is often less than men's because

a. women are less sociable than men.
b. women have no interests in common because they see each other as sexual competitors.
c. women remain at home, isolated from other women.
d. men prevent women from joining such groups.
e. women have so many opportunities to socialize that they have little need for common-interest associations.

7. In times of rapid social change,

a. common-interest associations decline in significance.
b. common-interest associations assume the roles and functions formerly held by kinship or age groups.
c. women form common-interest associations whereas men retain their membership in age and kinship groups.
d. men are able to adapt whereas women are not.
e. the role of the elderly becomes more important as the society adjusts to change.

8. A society composed of several groups that differ in their access to resources and prestige is said to be

a. stratified.
b. unfair.
c. immoral.
d. egalitarian.
e. open.

9. A/an _____ is a special form of social class in which membership is determined by birth and remains fixed for life.

a. clan
b. phratry
c. common-interest association
d. age group
e. caste

10. Symbolic indicators may not always be reliable in helping you assess someone's class status. Which of the following is an example of this?

a. A common form of recreation of lower-class males is playing pool at the local beer joint.
b. A con man from a lower-class background wears a tuxedo when he tries to sell you shares in a nonexistent corporation.
c. According to Emily Post, one can always identify upper-crust families by the presence of a day maid.
d. Demille O'Hara, striving to return to the simplicity of life as lived by his tribal ancestors, lets his day maid go.
e. *b* and *d*

11. The ability to change one's class position is known as

a. open class.
b. egalitarian.
c. mobility.
d. indicative of common-interest societies.
e. inevitable.

12. The degree of mobility in a stratified society is related to

a. the prevailing kind of family organization.
b. its ideology.
c. the number of different common-interest associations it has.
d. the difference between its richest and poorest classes.
e. genetic factors.

13. Which of the following could have contributed to the emergence of social stratification?

a. All human beings want to be looked up to by their fellow members of society.
b. Certain descent groups may have monopolized activities that turned out to play an important role in their society (such as propitiation of the gods in a horticultural society exposed to unpredictable weather).
c. An ethnic group with an economic or military advantage (such as knowledge of intensive agriculture or possession of firearms) that enters a foreign territory may become the ruling class within that area.
d. all of the above
e. none of the above

Answers to multiple-choice practice questions

1. b   2. b   3. d   4. a   5. b   6. e   7. b   8. a   9. e   10. e   11. c   12. a
13. d

True/False Practice Questions

1. Division of labor by sex is characteristic of all human societies.

2. Usually an increase in the number of common-interest associations is associated with urbanization, but these association are also found in traditional societies.

3. Castes are strongly exogamous.

4. Mobility refers to the ability to change one's class position.

5. An age grade is a group of people initiated into the group at the same time who move through the series of categories together.

Answers to true/false practice questions:

1. T   2. T   3. F   4. T   5. F

Practice Matching

Match the culture with its characteristic.

1. _____ Iroquois

2. _____ Tiriki

3. _____ New York Jews

4. _____ South Africans

5. _____ Maya

a. Cousins clubs in urban immigrant society

b. African nomadic pastoralists with an age set/age grade system

c. Castelike social organization based on racial divisions

d. Native Americans with separate but equal gender organization

e. Stratified society of pre-Columbian Central America

Answers to practice matching

1. d   2. b   3. a   4. c   5. e

Practice Essay

1. Marx felt that religion was "the opiate of the masses," claiming that it was often used by the upper classes to perpetuate their own hegemony. Can this perspective be applied to the Indian caste system? Would it be ethnocentric to do so?

2. Describe age grouping in Western society, using as an example the cousins clubs of North America.

Chapter 12
Political Organization and Social Control

Synopsis

Chapter 12 defines politics as a system that maintains social order within and between societies. Decentralized and centralized types of political systems are described and an attempt is made to define "law" in cross-cultural terms. The concepts of authority and legitimacy are discussed and various kinds of leadership are examined.

What You Should Learn from This Chapter

1. Know the four major kinds of political organization:
   • bands
   • tribes
   • chiefdoms
   • states
2. Understand how internal political and social control is maintained in different political systems.
3. Understand how external affairs are conducted in different political systems.
4. Understand how conflicts are resolved and the functions of law.
5. Recognize the impact of religion on social control.

Key Terms

political organization

uncentralized system

band

tribe

segmentary lineage system

centralized system

chiefdom

state

nation

sanctions

law

negotiation

mediation

adjudication

world view

Review Questions

1. What are the four basic kinds of political systems?

2. What kinds of societies typically have decentralized systems?

3. How is authority conferred in a band?

4. How is authority conferred in a tribe?

5. Distinguish between the segmentary lineage system and the clan.

6. What is the role of the leopard-skin chief of the Nuer?

7. What is the function of age-grade systems in the political structure of tribes?

8. Describe the role of the *tonowi* among the Kapauku Papuans.

9. What kinds of societies typically have centralized political systems?

10. Distinguish between nation and state.

11. What has women's role generally been in political leadership?

12. Describe women's role in Igbo society.

13. How is social control generally maintained in bands and tribes?

14. How do internalized controls guide behavior?

15. Distinguish between positive and negative sanctions.

16. Distinguish between informal and formal sanctions.

17. What are the limits on power in Bedouin society?

18. Why is the definition of law destined to be inexact?

19. What are the functions of law?

20. Differentiate between negotiation, adjudication, and mediation.

21. How are disputes handled by the Kpelle?

22. Why might warfare be so prominent in food-producing societies?

23. Compare the world view of the Abenaki with that of the Iroquois.

24. Distinguish between force and legitimacy.

25. In what ways is religion connected with politics?

Fill-in-the-Blank

1. The term _____ refers to the system of social relationships that is concerned with the maintenance of public order.

2. The term _____ refers to an administrative system having specialized personnel.

3. Anthropologists have identified four types of political systems; two are said to be _____ and two _____.

4. An egalitarian, autonomous small group composed of related people who occupy a single region is called a _____.

5. All humans were food foragers living in band-type organizations until about _____ years ago.

6. The _____ are an example of a society practicing band-level organization.

7. Most conflict in bands is settled by informal means, and decisions are usually made by _____.

8. A _____ is a larger grouping than a band and is linked to a specific territory.

9. A form of political organization in which a larger group is broken up into clans that are then divided into lineages, is called a _____ lineage system.

10. Among the Nuer, the tendency for widespread feuding to occur among lineages is counterbalanced by the actions of the _____.

11. In tribal societies of Melanesia, a type of leader called the _____ or *tonowi* is prevalent.

12. A _____ is a ranked society in which every member has a position in the hierarchy.

13. Chiefdoms are linked to _____ economic systems.

14. The Swazi have a _____ -level political system.

15. States are typically linked to _____ subsistence patterns.

16. An example of a society in which women play a notably strong political role is the _____.

17. The Wape of New Guinea use belief in _____ as a means of social control.

18. In North America we rely on both external and _____ controls to maintain social order.

19. Among the Bedouin _____ sanctions restrict the inappropriate use of power by those in authority.

20. The Inuit use _____ as a means of resolving conflict.

21. Malinowski distinguished law from _____ by whether there was a "definite social machinery of binding force."

22. Western societies make a distinction between _____ law, involving offenses committed against individuals, and _____ law, involving offenses committed against the state.

23. Disputes may be settled by _____, the use of direct argument and compromise by the disputing parties, or by _____, settlement through the assistance of an unbiased third party.

24. Warfare is most closely linked to the _____-type political system.

Exercises

I. Fill in the chart below, giving examples of each of the major types of political systems and describing their general characteristics. You can use this to study from later.

TYPES OF POLITICAL SYSTEMS

Type	Example	Characteristics
Band		
Tribe		
Chiefdom		
State		

172

II. Briefly identify and locate the following cultures.

1. Nuer

2. Kpelle

3. Igbo

4. Bedouin

5. Abenaki

6. Swazi

Multiple-Choice Practice Questions

1. The term "government" may be defined as

a. a kinship-based age set.
b. those aspects of social organization concerned with coordination and regulation of public behavior.
c. the informal leadership of a Ju/'hoansi hunter-gatherer band.
d. common-interest association focusing on political events.
e. an administrative system having specialized personnel.

2. Bands and tribes are both

a. centralized.
b. associated with industrialism.
c. dependent on age groups for political organization.
d. uncentralized and egalitarian.
e. hierarchical in social organization.

3. The form of social organization typical of hunter-gatherers is the _____, whereas horticulture and pastoralism are usually associated with the form of social organization called the _____.

a. tribe/chiefdom
b. tribe/state
c. tribe/band
d. band/chiefdom
e. band/tribe

4. The "leopard-skin chief" among the Nuer

a. is the head of the largest and most powerful clan.
b. is the head of the dominant matrilineage.
c. has the authority to force feuding lineages to accept "blood cattle" and stop feuding.
d. tries to mediate between feuding sides but does not have political power.
e. is the totem of one of the Nuer lineages.

174

5. Age-grade systems and common-interest associations are effective methods of integrating small autonomous units such as bands into larger social units. These methods may be described as _____ systems of political organization.

a. segmentary
b. negotiated
c. state
d. nonkinship
e. kinship

6. A _____ is a ranked society in which every member has a position in the hierarchy, and an individual's status is determined by membership in a descent group.

a. band
b. tribe
c. chiefdom
d. state
e. kindred

7. The state is distinctive in the extensiveness of its legitimate use of _____ to regulate the affairs of its citizens.

a. kinship
b. force
c. chiefs
d. religion
e. gossip

8. In a chiefdom, an individual's status is determined by membership in a

a. government.
b. social class.
c. bureaucracy.
d. descent group.
e. secret society.

9.   A cross-cultural comparison of systems of political organization reveals that

a.   many women who hold high office do so by virtue of their relationship to men.
b.   many women in positions of leadership adopt characteristics of temperament that are usually considered masculine.
c.   in many societies, women have as much political power as men.
d.   women may play an important role in political decisions even when they are not visible public leaders.
e.   all of the above

10. At the heart of political organization is

a.   control of unacceptable social behavior.
b.   the legitimate use of force to maintain order.
c.   unequal access to power.
d.   the dominance of males over females.
e.   the development of egalitarian relationships.

11. How is social order maintained in bands and tribes?

a.   public beatings
b.   murder carried on under cover of darkness
c.   occasional use of police and the court system
d.   threats of killing the first-born child
e.   gossip and fear of supernatural forces

12. Sanctions refer to

a.   internalized social controls.
b.   holy behavior.
c.   externalized social controls.
d.   decadent behavior.
e.   ritualized behavior.

13. _____ sanctions attempt to precisely and explicitly regulate people's behavior. They can be positive (such as military decorations) or negative (such as imprisonment).

a.   Hierarchical
b.   Egalitarian
c.   Informal
d.   Formal
e.   Magical

14. In centralized societies, antisocial behavior is usually dealt with in a court system by the use of formal, negative sanctions involving the application of abstract rules and the use of force. The primary aim is

a. to help the victim.
b. to renew social relations between the victim and the perpetrator of the crime.
c. to prevent witchcraft from being used.
d. to assign and punish guilt.
e. to provide a good show for the spectators.

15. The functions of law include

a. the definition of proper behavior in particular circumstances so that everyone is clear about their rights and duties.
b. allocating authority to use coercion to enforce sanctions.
c. redefining what is proper behavior when situations change.
d. all of the above
e. none of the above

16. A method of resolving disputes in which the disputing parties voluntarily arrive at a mutually satisfactory agreement is called

a. negotiation.
b. mediation.
c. adjudication.
d. use of sanctions.
e. law.

17. Which of the following are likely to be associated with warfare?

a. centralized political systems
b. the rise of cities
c. a technology that supports population growth
d. possession of complex, valuable property
e. all of the above

18. An exploitative world view is more likely to exist in which of the following technologies?

a. food foraging
b. horticulture
c. pastoralism
d. intensive agriculture
e. all of the above except a

19. Power based on force does not usually last very long; to be effective, it must be considered

a. legitimate.
b. mediated.
c. negotiated.
d. subject to sanctions.
e. inevitable.

Answers to multiple-choice practice questions

1. e   2. d   3. e   4. d   5. d   6. c   7. b   8. d   9. e   10. a   11. e   12. c
13. d   14. d   15. d   16. a   17. e   18. e   19. a

True/False Practice Questions

1. In the French monarchy under Louis XIV, the king *was* the state in an important sense.

2. Until recently many non-Western peoples had no fixed form of government in the sense that Westerners understand the term.

3. The Ju/'hoansi have a tribal-type political organization.

4. The Big Man of the Kapauku is called *tonowi*.

5. A classic example of a segmentary lineage system is found among the Nuer.

Answers to true/false practice questions

1. T   2. T   3. F   4. T   5. T

Practice Matching

Match the culture with its characteristic.

1. _____ Nuer

2. _____ Swazi

3. _____ Igbo

4. _____ Wape

5. _____ Abenaki

a. Nigerian society in which men and women occupy separate political spheres

b. Northeastern Native American foragers living in harmony with their environment

c. A southeast African state

d. A New Guinea people with effective informal and internalized controls

e. East African herders with a segmentary lineage system

Answers to practice matching:

1. e   2. c   3. a   4. d   5. b

Practice Essay

Why has the state-type system expanded to encompass most of the globe today? Explore how band, tribe, and chiefdom organizations might persist within a world order based primarily on states.

Chapter 13
Religion and the Supernatural

Synopsis

In Chapter 13 the text discusses the universality of religion, considering the functions served by religious belief and ritual in the social order. Various kinds of supernatural entities are compared and the relationships among magic, science, and religion are examined. The role of religion in culture change is also discussed.

What You Should Learn from This Chapter

1.
2.
3.
4.
5.

Key Terms and Names

religion

pantheon

Edward B. Tylor

Chapter 13
Religion and the Supernatural

Synopsis

In Chapter 13 the text discusses the universality of religion, considering the functions served by religious belief and ritual in the social order. Various kinds of supernatural beings are compared and the relationships among magic, science, and religion are examined. The role of religion in culture change is also discussed.

What You Should Learn from This Chapter

1. Understand why religion exists.
2. Understand the various forms of religious belief:
   • animatism
   • animism
   • shamanism
   • belief in ancestral spirits
   • belief in gods and goddesses
3. Understand the function of rites of passage and intensification.
4. Understand the relationship between religion, magic, and witchcraft and the functions of each.
5. Understand the role of religion in cultural change.

Key Terms and Names

religion

pantheon

Edward B. Tylor

animism

animatism

priest or priestess

shaman

rites of passage

rites of intensification

separation

transition

incorporation

imitative magic

contagious magic

witchcraft

divination

revitalization movements

Review Questions

1. What is the relationship between science and religion?

2. Why might there be less religion in more complex societies?

3. What are three categories of supernatural beings?

4. What is the role of gods and goddesses in many societies?

5. How does healing occur among the Ju/'hoansi?

6. What purpose do ancestral spirits serve?

7. In what type of society is one likely to find animism?

8. Distinguish between animism and animatism.

9. How does mana perpetuate itself?

10. In what type society is one likely to find priestesses?

11. How are shamans made and how do they carry out their work?

12. What benefits do people derive from enlisting the services of a shaman?

13. What are two main types of ritual?

14. What are the three stages in a rite of passage, according to Van Gennep?

15. Why are rites of intensification performed?

16. Distinguish between the two fundamental principles of magic.

17. In what ways does the Tewa origin myth reflect Tewa social structure?

18. How are witchhunts used for societal control?

19. What is the role of witchcraft among the Navajo?

20. What are the psychological functions of religion?

21. What are the social functions of religion?

22. How and why do revitalization movements emerge?

Fill-in-the-Blank

1. Alfonso Ortiz is an anthropologist of _____ ancestry who studied the religious beliefs of the Tewa.

2. In Tewa society the _____ mediate between the human and spiritual worlds and between the two moieties.

3. In the nineteenth century European thinkers believed that _____ would eventually eclipse religion.

4. The set of gods and goddesses in a society are called its _____.

5. In most societies with subsistence bases in _____ or _____, deities are conceptualized as masculine.

6. A belief that nature is animated by spirits is called _____.

7. A concept of impersonal power, such as mana, is called _____.

8. _____ are specialists who have acquired spiritual power, which they can use on behalf of human clients.

9. _____ was a pioneer in the study of rites of passage.

10. When Mende girls are initiated into adult society, they undergo _____.

11. A ceremony to bring rain to a drought-stricken community is a _____.

12. The three stages of a life crisis ritual are _____, _____, and _____.

13. _____ wrote *The Golden Bough*.

14. _____ magic is based on the assumption that things that are similar to each other have an effect on each other.

15. Assuming that a person's fingernail clippings, hair, blood, and so on retain a spiritual connection to that person is the basis for _____ magic.

16. Among the Navajo, _____ is a way of expression and channeling hostile feelings.

17. A _____ is a social movement whose intent is to totally transform a society.

18. Anthropologist _____ studied the stages typical of revitalization movements.

Exercise

Briefly identify and locate the following cultures discussed in the chapter.

1. Tewa

2. Sioux

3. Ibibio

4. Mende

Multiple-Choice Practice Questions

1. Islamic fundamentalism in Iran and Christian fundamentalism in the United States demonstrate that

   a. science has succeeded in destroying religion in the twentieth century.
   b. the nineteenth-century expectation that science would ultimately destroy religion is correct.
   c. science meets basic needs.
   d. religion is a powerful and dynamic force in society today.
   e. science is wrong.

2. _____ may be defined as the beliefs and patterns of behavior by which people try to control those aspects of the universe that are otherwise beyond their control.

   a. Political organization
   b. Government
   c. Kinship
   d. Common-interest associations
   e. Religion

3. Which of the following is LEAST likely to be extensively involved in religious beliefs and activities?

   a. single women with ten children living below the poverty line, who dropped out of school at age fourteen
   b. members of food-foraging societies with limited scientific knowledge
   c. peasants in a feudal society
   d. members of lower classes in an urban-industrial society
   e. wealthy members of urban-industrial societies with advanced scientific knowledge

4. A people's collection of gods and goddesses is called a

   a. mana.
   b. shaman.
   c. pantheon.
   d. priest.
   e. fetish.

5. Belief in a supreme being who controls the universe is usually associated with

a. bands.
b. tribes.
c. chiefdoms.
d. states.
e. multinational corporations.

6. If religious belief reflects the structure of society, in which types of society would you expect to find widespread belief in ancestral spirits?

a. those in which descent groups play a major role in social organization
b. those with a disproportionately large number of old people
c. those with a disproportionately large number of young people
d. those in which neolocal marital residence is the rule
e. those with egocentric systems such as the kindred

7. The belief that nature is animated with spirits is called

a. animation.
b. anima.
c. animatism.
d. animism.
e. ennui.

8. A _____ is a full-time religious specialist who occupies an office that has a certain rank and function.

a. shaman
b. priest
c. witch
d. magician
e. diviner

9. In acting as a healer, the shaman

a. provides reassurance to the community through an elaborate drama that may involve trickery.
b. may improve the patient's state of mind, which aids in recovery.
c. may be coping with his or her own problems by becoming intensely involved with the problems of others.
d. all of the above
e. none of the above

10. Ceremonies such as bar mitzvahs, elaborate wedding ceremonies, baby showers, and graduation parties that help individuals make major changes in their lives are referred to as rites of

a. transition.
b. intensification.
c. separation.
d. passage.
e. incorporation.

11. A funeral ceremony may be regarded as

a. a rite of passage.
b. an opportunity to restore the equilibrium of the group.
c. an opportunity for individuals to express their feelings in a structured way that ensures continuation of society.
d. a rite of intensification.
e. all of the above

12. In *The Golden Bough*, _____ distinguished between religion and magic.

a. Bronislaw Malinowski
b. Franz Boas
c. Sir James Frazer
d. Sir Edward Tylor
e. Clifford Geertz

13. Many magical incantations require the use of fingernail clippings of the intended victim. This is an example of

a. imitative magic.
b. contagious magic.
c. witch magic.
d. nightmare magic.
e. scientific thinking.

14. Magic involves the manipulation of powers for good or evil, whereas witchcraft involves the possession of an innate power used for

a. religious purposes.
b. scientific reasons.
c. evil.
d. traditional societies.
e. societies that lack religion.

15. Religion, magic, and witchcraft are all SIMILAR in which of the following ways?

a. They all disappear once modern education and scientific training expand.
b. They all share the common goal of improving social relationships within a community.
c. They are all associated with morose nonconformists who try to destroy society.
d. They provide explanations of events and are mechanisms of social control.
e. They are all morally neutral.

16. A belief in _____ enables people to explain why things go wrong by blaming certain individuals who are said to have the internal psychic ability to cause harm to others.

a. witchcraft
b. magic
c. divination
d. contagion
e. evil

17. Which of the following illustrate the psychological functions of religion?

a. Among the Holy Ghost People of the United States, handling snakes and drinking strychnine is a common feature of their worship; one explanation of this behavior is that by confronting the possibility of death, they achieve a sense of awe and transcendence.
b. An Islamic judge who orders the hand of a thief cut off can sleep soundly at night because he thinks of himself as merely the agent of divinely inspired justice.
c. The Tewa Indian origin myth provides every Tewa with a sense of his place in an orderly universe.
d. all of the above
e. none of the above

18. A _____ is a deliberate effort by members of a society to construct a more satisfying culture.

a. divination
b. rite of intensification
c. fetish
d. segmentary lineage system
e. revitalization movement

19. Which of the following statements about revitalization movements is INCORRECT?

a. The purpose of revitalization movements is to reform society.
b. Revitalization movements always fail because they require too much change to be tolerated.
c. All known major religions, including Judaism, Christianity, and Islam, began as revitalization movements.
d. Revitalization movements may be completely unrealistic.
e. Revitalization movements may be adaptive and give rise to long-lasting religions.

Answers to multiple-choice practice questions

1. d   2. e   3. e   4. c   5. d   6. a   7. d   8. b   9. d   10. d   11. e   12. c
13. b   14. c   15. d   16. a   17. d   18. e   19. b

True/False Practice Questions

1. The belief that nature is animated by spirits is called animism.

2. Rituals reinforce social solidarity and thus enable individuals and groups to get through a crisis.

3. Rites of intensification help individuals get through a crisis.

4. Religion provides an orderly model of the universe and reduces fear and anxiety.

Answers to true/false practice questions

1. T   2. T   3. F   4. T

Practice Matching

Match the culture with its characteristic.

1. _____ Navajo

    a. West African people who practice a female initiation rite involving clitoridectomy

2. _____ Tewa

    b. Southwestern Native Americans with a witchcraft tradition

3. _____ Ibibio

    c. Native Americans of the plains who started the Ghost Dance as a religious revitalization

4. _____ Sioux

    d. Native Americans of New Mexico whose origin myth reflects and validates their social structure

5. _____ Mende

    e. Sub-Saharan African people with a witchcraft tradition

Answers to practice matching

1. b   2. d   3. e   4. c   5. a

Practice Essay

Bronislaw Malinowski, in his classic essay *Magic, Science and Religion*, claimed that each of these was a viable mode of cognition and that most societies exhibit all of them in variable proportions. In what ways does magical thinking persist in contemporary North America? Is it likely to persist into the future?

Chapter 14
The Arts

Synopsis

Chapter 14 examines the ethnocentric assumptions implicit in most Western definitions of the arts and artists. It distinguishes different types of creative activity such as the verbal arts, music, and sculpture and attempts to come up with a cross-culturally valid definition of art.

What You Should Learn from This Chapter

1. Understand why anthropologists are interested in the arts.
2. Understand the forms of verbal arts and how they function in society:
   • myth
   • legend
   • tale
3. Understand the function of music.
4. Understand the range of visual and plastic arts in human societies.

Key Terms

folklore

folkloristics

myth

legend

epic

tale

motif

ethnomusicology

tonality

entopic phenomena

construal

iconic images

Review Questions

1. Distinguish between secular and religious art.

2. What are the basic kinds of verbal arts studied by anthropologists?

3. Give an example of how myth expresses the world view of a people.

4. Distinguish between legend and myth.

5. Why is matriarchy a common theme in many societies' myths?

6. What role does poetry play in the lives of the Bedouins?

7. What type of society is likely to have epics? Why?

8. What aspects of legends are of interest to anthropologists?

9. Why are anthropologists interested in tales?

10. What are the functions of music?

11. What is sculpture?

12. Distinguish between art and craft.

13. Describe West African scluture and its role in society.

14. What might the masks of Africa symbolize?

15. What is the importance of entopic phenomena?

16. What is the "second stage" of trance?

17. Are there any universal characteristics of art?

Fill-in-the-Blank

1. The term "verbal arts" is preferred to the term _____, a term developed in the nineteenth century to refer to traditional oral stories of European peasants.

2. The word "myth," in _____ usage, refers to something that is widely believed to be true but isn't.

3. Tabaldak and Odziozo are characters in the origin myth of the _____.

4. Legends are _____ narratives that recount the deeds of heroes, the movements of peoples, and the establishment of customs.

5. Studies of tales in the southeast United States now indicate that they originated in _____ rather than Europe.

6. "Little songs" that occur every day were studied among the _____.

7. The study of music in its cultural setting is called _____.

8. The term _____ is used to refer to scale systems and their modifications in music.

9. An alternative to the Western octave system is the _____, which is defined by five equidistant tones.

10. Two people playing different patterns of beats at the same time is called _____.

11. The cultures of _____ have a particularly rich tradition of sculpture.

12. Among the Pomo Indians of California, _____ is an important expression of aesthetic interest.

13. The human nervous sytem produces images out of which patterns are construed. These are called _____.

Multiple-Choice Practice Questions

1. Whether useful or nonuseful, all art is an expression of

a. the innate need to be impractical.
b. a fundamental human capacity for religious expression.
c. state-level societies that can afford specialists.
d. political domination of minorities by elites.
e. the symbolic representation of form and the expression of feeling that constitutes creativity.

2. The observation that all cultures include activities that provide aesthetic pleasure suggests that

a. humans may have an innate or acquired need to produce art.
b. the human mind requires the stimulation of imaginative play to prevent boredom.
c. all societies, from food-foraging bands to industrial states, include art in their culture.
d. art is a necessary activity in which all normal, active members of society participate.
e. all of the above

3. Anthropologists prefer to use the term *verbal arts* rather than the term *folklore* because the term

a. *folklore* is used only by linguists; the term *verbal arts* is used only by anthropologists.
b. *verbal arts* sounds more sophisticated.
c. *verbal arts* is more scientific.
d. *folklore* implies lack of sophistication and is a condescending term to use.
e. *folklore* refers only to fairy tales.

4. The type of verbal arts that has received the most study and attention is

a. poetry.
b. incantations.
c. narrative.
d. proverbs.
e. riddles.

5. The word "myth" as used by anthropologists differs somewhat from the popular conception of the term. As used in popular parlance, "myth" means

a. a scientific explanation for the origin of the universe.
b. a widely believed falsehood (e.g., "It's a myth that if a pregnant woman eats strawberries her child will be born with a strawberry-colored birthmark").
c. a narrative that provides a rationale for religious beliefs and practices.
d. an expression of the world view of a people.
e. an explanatory description of an orderly universe.

6. In the myth of Tabaldak and Odziozo, Tabaldak first created the Abenakis from stone and then from living wood. What does this tell us about the functions of myths?

a. Myths function to tell actual history; the Abenakis believe that they were originally made of wood.
b. Myths bring humor into the lives of the Abenakis because the myths are so ridiculous.
c. Myths function primarily to provide entertainment; the Abenakis know they were not made from wood, but like to tell this story to visiting anthropologists who are so gullible.
d. Myths function to express a culture's world view; the Abenakis see themselves as belonging to the world of living things rather than to the nonliving world of stone.
e. Myths provide skills of woodworking and stonemasonry to the Abenakis.

7. Because legends contain details of a people's past, they are a form of history; because they often give a picture of a people's view of the world and humanity's place in it, they are like

a. poetry.
b. religion.
c. magic.
d. kinship systems.
e. myths.

8. When an anthropologist uses the term _____, he or she is referring to a category of verbal narratives that are secular, nonhistorical, and seen primarily as a source of entertainment.

a. "folklore"
b. "myth"
c. "tale"
d. "legend"
e. "drama"

9. Your text describes a type of narrative found in many cultures in which a peasant father and his son, while traveling with their beast of burden, meet a number of people who criticize them. What is the motif?

a. The "motif" refers to the psychological motives of the characters in a story, in this case the desire of the son to do better than his father.
b. "Motif" means the historical background to the story, in this case the history of exploitation of the peasantry.
c. The "motif" refers to the story situation, in this case a father and son trying to please everyone.
d. "Motif" means the physical environment in which the story occurs, in this case the yam gardens of Ghana.
e. The "motif" refers to the economic background, in this case feudalism.

10. The "little songs" of the Bedouin are considered un-Islamic; they are the discourse of children, used to express rebellious ideas and feelings. Thus they are

a. antistructural.
b. forbidden.
c. sung among Europeans only.
d. sung only when the Bedouins are away from their homeland.
e. sung only at marriages.

11. The field of ethnomusicology

a. is concerned with human music rather than natural music.
b. is the study of music in its cultural setting.
c. began in the nineteenth century with the collection of folksongs.
d. concerns the organization of melody, rhythm, and form in a culture's music.
e. all of the above

12. Scale systems and their modifications in music are called

a. tonality.
b. ethnomusicology.
c. sculpture.
d. verbal arts.
e. pentatonic.

13. During the Washington Peace March in the sixties, thousands of people sang the song "We Shall Overcome." This song expressed a feeling of common purpose to counteract repression and to reform society. It created a sense of unity among the diverse members of the crowd. This example illustrates the _____ of music.

a. social functions
b. geographical distribution
c. tonality
d. mythological features
e. polyrhythms

14. Objects that are trivial, low in symbolic content, or impermanent are usually considered products of

a. an ethnomusicologist.
b. a tale.
c. craft.
d. art.
e. sculpture.

15. To understand the symbolic significance of an art work in West Africa, the anthropologist

a. must speak to the individual artist, who is the only one who knows what was intended by the art work.
b. must learn to be an artist.
c. can ask anyone in the culture, because the art follows cultural conventions and has a certain symbolic significance for the group.
d. must study something else besides art, because it is impossible to explain to an outsider.
e. must study art in other cultures.

Answers to multiple-choice practice questions

1. e   2. e   3. d   4. c   5. b   6. d   7. e   8. c   9. c   10. a   11. e   12. a
13. a   14. c   15. c

True/False Practice Questions

1. The term "tale" refers to a type of narrative that is secular, nonhistorical, and seen primarily as a source of entertainment.

2. Legends are semihistorical narratives which recount the deeds of heroes, the movement of peoples and the establishment of local customs.

3. The word "myth," in popular usage, refers to something that is widely believed to be true but probably isn't.

4. Legends provide clues as to what is considered appropriate behavior in a culture.

Answers to true/false practice questions

1. T   2. T   3. T   4. T

Practice Essay

Many famous biographies or novels about artists in the West stress the individual creativity of the artist (for example, James Joyce's *Portrait of the Artist as a Young Man*). Artists are portrayed as people who have the vision to rise above and beyond the social and cultural conditions into which they were born, sometimes even crossing the boundaries of normality as typically defined by society. How is this vision of the artist different from the conception of artists held by non-Western societies?

Chapter 15
Cultural Change

Synopsis

Chapter 15 disusses the mechanisms of cultural change and examines anthropology's role in the changes sweeping the world. The use of the term "modernization" is considered from a cross-cultural perspective.

What You Should Learn from This Chapter

1. Understand how cultures change and the mechanisms involved:
   • innovation
   • diffusion
   • cultural loss
   • acculturation
2. Understand why the field of applied anthropology developed.
3. Understand how societies react to forcible change:
   • syncretism
   • revitalization movements
4. Understand the process of modernization and its effect on societies.

Key Terms and Names

primary innovation

secondary innovation

diffusion

acculturation

genocide

applied anthropology

Franz Boas

syncretism

nativistic (revivalistic) movement

millenarism

modernization

structural differentiation

revolutionary

integrative mechanisms

tradition

Review Questions

1. Distinguish between primary and secondary innovation.

2. Provide an example of primary innovation.

3. Why is it that cultural context provides the means for innovation to occur?

4. What things have European Americans borrowed from American Indians?

5. What is meant by cultural loss?

6. Describe the nature of acculturation.

7. What three factors seem to be underlying causes of genocide?

8. What does the field of applied anthroplogy attempt to accomplish?

9. How did the Trobriand Islanders react to the British game of cricket?

10. What is the purpose of revitalization movements?

11. What are the precipitators of rebellion and revolution?

12. What is the problem with the term "moderization"?

13. What are the four subprocesses of modernization?

14. What is meant by the "culture of discontent"?

Fill-in-the-Blank

1. Innovations based on the chance discovery of some new principle are called
   _____ innovations, while innovations resulting from the deliberate application of
   these principles are called _____ innovations.

2. The spread of customs or practices from one culture to another is called _____.

3. According to Ralph Linton, as much as _____ percent of a culture's content is due
   to borrowing.

4. _____ occurs when groups with different cultures come into intensive, firsthand
   contact and one or both groups experience massive cultural changes.

5. One society may retain its culture but lose its autonomy, becoming a _____ within
   the dominant culture.

6. The extermination of one people by another is called _____.

7. The field of _____ anthropology uses anthropological knowledge and techniques
   for practical purposes.

8. The applied work of anthropologist _____ helped reform the U.S. government's
   immigration policies.

9. Under conditions of acculturation, indigenous populations may blend foreign traits with those
   of their own culture to form a new cultural system. This response is called _____.

10. The Trobrianders blended indigenous traditions with the British game of _____.

11. _____ movements are deliberate attempts by members of a society to construct a
    more satisfactory culture.

12. A revitalization movement that attempts to bring back a destroyed but not forgotten way of life
    is called a _____ or revivalistic movement.

13. A revitalization movement that attempts to resurrect a suppressed, outcast group that has its
    own special subcultural ideology and has occupied an inferior social position for a long time is
    called _____.

14. Revolutions have occurred only during the last _____ years, since the
    emergence of centralized systems of political authority.

15. Modernization refers to the process of cultural and socioeconomic change whereby developing
    societies become more similar to _____ industrialized societies.

16. The _____ aspect of modernization means a shift in population from rural areas to cities.

17. The Skolt Lapps in the country of _____ traditionally supported themselves by fishing and reindeer herding.

18. The Shuar Indians promoted cooperative _____ ranching as their new economic base.

19. By the early 1970s the United States, encompassing 6 percent of the world's population, was consuming about _____ percent of the world's output of copper, coal and oil.

20. The Wauja are a community of indigenous people whose claim to certain lands and the ceremonies that take place there are threatened by _____ and _____.

Exercise

Briefly identify and locate the following cultures.

1. Skolt Lapps

2. Shuar

3. Haitians

4. Wauja

Multiple-Choice Practice Questions

1. In New England, the culture of English speakers replaced the various cultures of Native Americans living along the coast. Your text says that this occurred because

   a. English-speaking culture was superior to Native American culture.
   b. Native American culture was superior to English-speaking culture.
   c. it is inevitable that Englishspeakers will replace other cultures that they encounter.
   d. a combination of accidental factors contributed to the success of English speakers in establishing colonies along coastal New England.
   e. the success of English speakers was only a temporary setback for the progressive development of Native American culture.

2. The chance discovery of some new principle that can be applied in a variety of ways is called

   a. primary innovation.
   b. primary syncretism.
   c. applied anthropology.
   d. millenarism.
   e. diffusion.

3. The deliberate use of basic ideas in some practical application, such as making use of the knowledge of how electricity works to develop the telephone, is called

   a. revitalization.
   b. millenarism.
   c. modernization.
   d. integrative mechanism.
   e. secondary innovation.

4. Copernicus's discovery that the earth orbits the sun rather than vice versa

   a. was a primary innovation that met the cultural goals and needs of his time.
   b. was a primary innovation that was out of step with the needs, values, and goals of his time.
   c. was a secondary innovation that put into application the discovery by Ptolemy that heavenly bodies moved on crystalline spheres around the earth.
   d. was a secondary innovation that was deliberately developed by Copernicus to destroy the Polish Church.
   e. resulted from diffusion of ideas from India.

5. According to the North American anthropologist Ralph Linton, about 90 percent of any culture's content comes from

a. primary innovation.
b. diffusion.
c. invention.
d. syncretism.
e. revolution.

6. In biblical times, chariots and carts were widespread in the Middle East, but by the sixth century the roads had deteriorated so much that wheeled vehicles were replaced by camels. This illustrates that cultural change is sometimes due to

a. primary invention.
b. secondary invention.
c. diffusion.
d. revitalization.
e. cultural loss.

7. As a result of prolonged firsthand contact between societies A and B, which of the following might happen?

a. The cultures of A and B might fuse, becoming a single culture with elements of both.
b. Society A might retain its distinctive culture but lose its autonomy and come to survive as a subculture such as a caste or ethnic group.
c. Society A might be wiped out by society B, with only a few scattered refugees living as members of the dominant society.
d. all of the above
e. none of the above

8. The extermination of one group of people by another, often deliberately and in the name of progress, is called

a. genocide.
b. acculturation.
c. diffusion.
d. applied anthropology.
e. primary innovation.

9. The field of applied anthropology developed

a. through efforts to help the poor in North American society.
b. in sociology classrooms.
c. in industry.
d. in colonial situations.
e. through the efforts of women opposed to prohibition.

10. In acculturation, subordinate groups will often incorporate new cultural elements into their own culture, creating a blend of old and new; a reinterpretation of new cultural elements to fit them with already existing traditions is called

a. syncretism.
b. innovation.
c. diffusion.
d. integrative mechanisms.
e. modernization.

11. A deliberate attempt by members of society to construct a more satisfying culture may be called

a. a secondary innovation.
b. a revitalization movement.
c. an enervating movement.
d. syncretism.
e. a primary innovation.

12. A revitalization movement in which a suppressed group believes that it will eventually change its inferior position to become superior is

a. a revivalistic movement.
b. revolutionary.
c. millenaristic.
d. nativistic.
e. syncretism.

13. Which of the following is/are considered to be important precipitators of rebellion and revolution?

a. A sudden reversal of recent economic advances
b. The media no longer support the government.
c. The established leadership loses prestige.
d. A strong, charismatic leader organizes attacks on the existing government.
e. all of the above

14. The term "modernization"

a. is a relativistic rather than ethnocentric concept.
b. refers to the process of cultural and socioeconomic change whereby societies acquire the characteristics of industrialized societies.
c. refers to a global and all-encompassing process whereby modern cities gradually deteriorate.
d. can be used to show that all societies go through the same stages of evolutionary development, culminating in the urban-industrial state.
e. is not used by anthropologists.

15. As modernization occurs, which of the following changes are likely to follow?

a. Literacy increases.
b. Religion decreases.
c. Kinship plays a less significant role.
d. Social mobility increases.
e. all of the above

16. The division of a single role (which serves several functions) into two or more roles (each with a single specialized function) is called

a. millenarization.
b. modernization.
c. structural differentiation.
d. industrialization.
e. diffusion.

17. Changes in Skolt Lapp society occurred because

a. men switched from reindeer herding to other sources of income.
b. the number of reindeer declined.
c. snowmobiles were used to herd reindeer.
d. society became hierarchical.
e. women became more powerful than men.

Answers to multiple-choice practice questions

1. d   2. a   3. e   4. b   5. b   6. e   7. d   8. a   9. d   10. a   11. b   12. c
13. e   14. b   15. e   16. c   17. c

Practice Matching

Match the culture with its characteristic.

1. _____ Skolt Lapps

2. _____ Shuar

3. _____ Wauja

4. _____ Iranians

5. _____ Tasmanians

a. Established an Islamic government after a successful religious revitalization

b. An Amazonian people who mobilized to protect their native lands

c. Native Americans of Ecuador who formed a federation to protect their interests

d. Arctic Scandinavians whose society was radically changed by the introduction of snowmobiles

e. Indigenous people off the coast of Australia who were wiped out by Europeans

Answers to practice matching

1. d   2. b   3. c   4. a   5. e

Practice Essays

1. Describe the impact of modernization on Skolt Lapps, Shuar Indians, and Wauja.

2. In what ways can the rising tide of Islamic fundamentalism in the Middle East and other areas of the world be seen as a revitalization movement? Are there other terms from the chapter that could apply to this phenomenon? What might anthropology contribute to our understanding of such movements?

Chapter 16
The Future of Humanity

Synopsis

In this concluding chapter the text considers the role of anthropological knowledge in facing the world of the future.

What You Should Learn from This Chapter

1. Understand the contribution anthropology can make in planning for humanity's future.
2. Understand what a one-world culture is and the feasibility of such a system.
3. Consider the problems facing humankind and some possible avenues of solution.

Key Terms

cultural pluralism

structural violence

replacement reproduction

one-world culture

217

ethnic resurgence

global apartheid

"culture of discontent"

Review Questions

1. What shortcomings are evident in future-oriented literature?

2. What makes anthropologists uniquely suited to contribute to planning for the future?

3. Can the globe today be described as a "one-world culture"?

4. Why are predictions of a politically integrated world probably incorrect?

218

5. Give an example of how misunderstandings might actually increase in a one-world culture.

6. Give some contemporary examples of ethnic resurgence.

7. How does the concept of ethnocentrism interfere with cultural pluralism?

8. In what way is the world system one of "global apartheid"?

9. Provide examples of structural violence.

10. What is thought to be the immediate cause of world hunger? Provide examples.

11. Why is the suggestion that countries adopt agricultural practices similar to the United States not necessarily sound advice?

12. What is meant by the "exploitative world view"?

13. In what way is contemporary North American culture one of "discontent"?

Fill-in-the-Blank

1. Anthropologists try to be _____, meaning they take into account many interacting factors to understand the functioning of the complex whole.

2. Anthropologists have a _____, meaning they take a long-term view of things.

3. Over the past five thousand years, political units have grown steadily _____ in size and _____ in number.

4. All large states have a tendency to _____.

5. There are about _____ recognized states in the world today, but three to five thousand national groups.

6. An important force for global unity are the _____ corporations that cut across national boundaries.

7. The separation of whites and blacks in South Africa under the domination of the white minority was a system called _____.

8. About _____ of the population of the world is nonwhite.

9. A great deal of the violence in the world is not due to the unique and personal decisions of individuals but to social, political, and economic conditions; this is referred to as _____ violence.

10. The population of the world today is about _____.

11. The cause of world hunger is not so much the ability to produce food but the ability to _____ it effectively.

12. _____ rain, caused in part by smokestack gases, is causing damage to lakes, forests, and ground water.

13. All civilizations have an _____ world view that tends to promote ecologically unsound cultural practices.

14. Replacement reproduction refers to a rate of reproduction in which a couple have no more than _____ children.

Multiple-Choice Practice Questions

1. Most people plan for the future by looking at trends in

   a. ancient history.
   b. hemlines.
   c. third-world countries.
   d. food supplies.
   e. recent history.

2. Anthropologists are trained to develop effective predictions of the future because they are

   a. holistic in perspective.
   b. good at seeing how parts fit together into a larger whole.
   c. trained to have an evolutionary perspective.
   d. able to see short-term trends in longer-term perspective.
   e. all of the above

3. Over the past five thouand years, political units have

   a. grown steadily smaller in size.
   b. grown steadily larger in size and fewer in number.
   c. eliminated multinational corporations.
   d. promoted individual freedoms.
   e. eliminated slavery

4. Multinational corporations

   a. have been widespread in Western culture since medieval times.
   b. were very common during the colonial period.
   c. have become a major force in the world today since the 1950s.
   d. have been disintegrating since the 1950s.
   e. promote relativistic rather than ethnocentric ideas.

5. Which of the following expresses the NEGATIVE consequences of multinational corporations on the international and domestic scenes?

a. Multinational corporations cross-cut nations and thus achieve a global unity.
b. Multinational corporations have become a major force in the world since the 1950s.
c. Multinational corporations have become so powerful that they have been able to influence government decisions so that they benefit the company rather than the people.
d. Multinational corporations are products of the technological revolution.
e. They have developed sophisticated data-processing techniques that enable them to keep track of worldwide operations.

6. Cultural pluralism

a. may constitute a temporary stage in a process of integration into a single melting-pot culture.
b. implies the absence of bigotry and racism.
c. implies respect for the cultural traditions of other peoples.
d. may result from conquest or from several culturally distinct groups occupying an area that eventually becomes unified as a larger political entity.
e. all of the above

7. Which of the following represent the NEGATIVE consequences of ethnocentrism?

a. By believing that another culture is inferior to yours, you can, with a sense of righteousness, destroy its temples, cottage industry, polygynous practices, and so on in order to bring it into line with your culture's standards of appropriate behavior and belief.
b. Ethnocentrism confers a sense of pride in and loyalty to one's own cultural traditions.
c. Ethnocentrism provides a feeling of psychological gratification that one is living the right kind of life.
d. Ethnocentrism contributes to a sense of personal worth.
e. Ethnocentrism strengthens social solidarity.

8. "Global apartheid" refers to

a. the prediction that in the future, South Africa will dominate the world economy.
b. the fact that whites, although they make up only one-third of the world's population today, have greater access to the world's resources.
c. the fact that nonwhites suffer a disproportionate share of the world's problems of hunger, pollution, and overpopulation and have a much greater chance of dying a violent death than do whites.
d. the fact that the structure of world society is very similar to that of South Africa.
e. all of the above except *a*

9. _____ is violence produced by social, political, and economic structures rather than by the unique and personal decisions of individuals.

a. Torture
b. Modernization
c. Structural violence
d. Insanity
e. Religion

10. The change from subsistence farming to cash crops

a. enables farmers to enlarge their holdings and feed their families more effectively.
b. results in the relocation of subsistence farmers to urban areas or to lands ecologically unfit for farming.
c. leads to the decline of multinational corporations.
d. supports cultural pluralism.
e. leads to revitalization.

11. An Asian wet-rice farmer might choose not to adopt North American techniques of intensive agriculture because

a. he or she cannot afford to buy the chemical products typically used in this type of agriculture.
b. the North American method requires at least eight calories of energy to be expended for every calorie produced, whereas the wet-rice farmer produces three hundred calories for every calorie he or she invests.
c. the North American method produces toxic substances that destroy delicate ecological balances.
d. he or she predicts that the North American method, while successful for a short period of time, is sowing the seeds of its own destruction.
e. all of the above

12. Pollution, although a worldwide consequence of certain agricultural and industrial activities, is more of a problem in _____ because chemicals that may be banned in richer nations can be used more easily.

a. poor countries
b. industrialized countries
c. arctic countries
d. Mediterranean countries
e. ocean areas

13. If a country achieves "replacement reproduction," this means that

a. no one can be born without someone else dying.
b. each reproductive couple has no more children.
c. its population will immediately stop growing.
d. its population will continue to grow for another sixty years.
e. every other generation can have children.

Answers to multiple choice practice questions

1. e   2. e   3. b   4. c   5. c   6. e   7. a   8. e   9. c   10. b   11. e   12. a
13. d

True/False Practice Questions

1. Multinational corporations have constituted a strong force for global unity.

2. Structural violence refers to violence produced by social, political, and economic structures rather than by the unique and personal decisions of individuals.

3. The change from subsistence farming to cash crops leads to economic improvement in countries that made the change.

4. Modernization refers to a situation in which groups with different ways of acting and thinking can interact socially with mutual respect.

Answers to true/false practice questions

1. T   2. T   3. F   4. F

Practice Essay

The effort to reduce population growth faces enormous cultural obstacles. Illustrate this by describing Chinese efforts to promote one-child families, and consider whether Western planners should attempt to encourage similar efforts in the Islamic world, where birth control is prohibited on religious grounds. Where does appropriate global planning run up against the charge of ethnocentrism or cultural imperialism?